A CORNISH CHORUS

Photo : W. R. Harvey

POLPERRO

" Dreaming, I watch
  While my thoughts like the seabirds
  Cleave to the water
  Or soar to the sunlight . . .

  Staying to gaze
  That the magic impression.
  May live in remembrance
  For nurture and solace
  In the slow seasons
  Of exile that wait me."   ARTHUR L. SALMON.

A CORNISH CHORUS

A Collection of Prose and Verse

EDITED BY
MURIEL HAWKEY

WITH A PREFACE BY
J. C. TREWIN

LONDON :
WESTAWAY BOOKS LTD.
1948

Sole Export Agents - *Staples Press, Ltd.*
LONDON

First published in 1948

Printed by
The Devonshire Press, Higher Fleet Street, Torquay,
England

ACKNOWLEDGMENTS

GRATEFUL thanks are due to the following for permission to publish certain copyright material in this Anthology : C. C. Abbott and Messrs. Jonathan Cape Ltd. for poem from *The Sandcastle and Other Poems ;* Frances Bellerby and Messrs. Peter Davies Ltd. for poems from *Plash Mill ;* John Betjeman and Messrs. John Murray for poem from *New Bats in Old Belfries* and for poems from *Old Lights for New Chancels ;* Margaret Bone for poems ; Joseph Braddock for a poem ; Mrs. Byles for poem by the late C. E. Byles from *Cornish Breakers ;* Messrs. Wm. Blackwood & Sons Ltd. for an extract from a poem by William Canton from *A Lost Epic ;* Sir E. K. Chambers for a poem ; Elizabeth J. Coatsworth for a poem ; John Davidson and The Richards Press for a poem ; Walter de la Mare and Messrs. Faber & Faber Ltd. for poems from *Collected Poems of Walter de la Mare* and from *Collected Rhymes and Verses ;* Richard Steele & Son for poems by the late Crosbie Garstin ; Joyce Grenfell and the *Observer* for a poem ; Geoffrey Grigson and Messrs. Routledge & Kegan Paul for a poem from *Under the Cliff and Other Poems ;* The Trustees of the Hardy Estate and Messrs. Macmillan & Co. Ltd. for poems from *Collected Poems of Thomas Hardy ;* Lorna L. Hawkey for poems ; M. Lawry Hawkey for poems ; W. P. Hodgkinson for *The Under Road ;* Gladys Hunkin for poems ; Miss Isabella Johnson for poems by the late Lionel Johnson ; Sinclair Lewis and Messrs. Jonathan Cape Ltd. for extract from *Ann Vickers ;* P. H. B. Lyon for a poem ; Bernard Moore for four poems ; R. Morton Nance for the Cornish translation of Bernard Moore's *Cornish Hymn ;* Messrs. Macmillan & Co. Ltd. for two passages from *Highways and Byways of Devon and Cornwall* by Arthur H. Norway ; J. H. B. Peel for a poem ; J. H. B. Peel and Messrs. Venturebooks Ltd. for a poem from *Frost at Midnight ;* J. H. B. Peel and Messrs. Chaterson Ltd. for extract from *Mere England;* The Executors of the late Mary Vosper Prior for poems ; Foy F. Quiller-Couch for poems by the late Sir A. T. Quiller-Couch ; M. E. Rhodes and the Proprietors of *Punch* for a poem ; C. C. Rogers, now writing as C. C. Vyvyan, and Messrs. John Lane the Bodley Head Ltd., London, for a passage from *Echoes in Cornwall* and two passages from *Cornish Silhouettes;* Peter Rowlands for a poem ; A. L. Rowse and Messrs. Faber & Faber Ltd. for poem from *Poems of a Decade ;* two poems from *Poems Chiefly Cornish ;* and two poems from *Poems of Deliverance;* Earl Russell for extract from *The Scientific Outlook ;* Arthur L. Salmon for poems ; A.S. (Mrs. Pearson) and the *Observer* for two poems ; Edward Shanks for a poem ; L. A. G. Strong for a poem ; Netherton & Worth Ltd. for poem by Bishop C. W. Stubbs from *Truro Carol Book ;* Messrs. Wm. Heinemann Ltd. for poem from *Collected Poems of A. C. Swinburne* and for extract from *Tristram of Lyonnesse* by A. C. Swinburne ; The Macmillan Company, New York, for their permission to use a poem by Sara Teasdale from *Dark of the Moon* (copyright 1926) ; J. C. Tregarthen and Messrs. John Murray for extracts from *Wild Life at the Land's End ;* Anne Treneer for poems ; J. C. Trewin for poems ; Messrs. John Lane the Bodley Head Ltd. for extracts from *Unknown Cornwall* by C. E. Vulliamy and for poem by Rex Warner from *Poems and Contradictions ;* Margaret Willy for a poem ; Margaret Willy and Messrs. Chaterson Ltd. for poem from *The Invisible Sun ;* and Messrs. Jonathan Cape for poem by Andrew Young from *The Green Man.*

Every effort has been made to trace copyright owners. Apologies are tendered in advance to proprietors and publishers concerned if any copyright material has been included for which, due to inability to trace the present owners, permission has not been specifically granted.

LIST OF ILLUSTRATIONS AT END OF TEXT

CONTENTS

CONTENTS—*continued*

CONTENTS—*continued*

CONTENTS—*continued*

CONTENTS—*continued*

CONTENTS—*continued*

PREFACE

WHEN I saw Muriel Hawkey's manuscript I turned to find what she had chosen for the part of Cornwall most dear to me. She knows it well ; at one period we lived within twelve miles of each other in the far south. Here, gathered in her pages, are the sights and sounds of that peninsula at a peninsula's end, the Lizard's all-but-island. We go from the east, with Helford River

> *Streaming*
>
> *By Durgan to the sea ;*

southward past Cadgwith, where Lionel Johnson marked " the gulls' curving flight across the black-girt bay " ; on by the " glittering rocks " of the Lizard promontory (Nicholas Mitchell had the right epithet) ; westward to the cliffs of which Robert Hunt wrote in high-Romantick excitement :

> *Kynance Cove, whose awful steep*
>
> *In terror lives,*

and so around past Helston, the dance in our ears, into the central curve of Mount's Bay, and to that shore

> *Where the great Vision of the guarded mount*
>
> *Looks towards Namancos and Bayona's hold.*

Certainly, then, the book has the south in its eyes. Where next ? Farther westward to the Land's End itself : Humphry Davy " illumes the dark Bolerium, seat of storms." By Sennen the Gwynvyr sounds. And the Isles of Scilly, the Cornish Hesperides ? What of the flower-islands in their summer-sea (or, if you prefer, Shelley's " storm-encompassed isles ") ? The anthologist has remembered : Crosbie Garstin ishere, and in the first verse of " The Sea Lights " two strong magics meet :

Flashed Lizard to Bishop
" They're rounding the fish up
Close under my cliffs where the cormorants nest,
The lugger lamps glitter
In hundreds and litter
The sea-floor like spangles. What news from the West ?"

Properly, in another manner, Walter de la Mare is in full
incantation in " Sunk Lyonesse " where

> *the unearthly lovely weep*
> *In lament of the music they make*
> *In the sullen courts of sleep.*

Lyonesse (however you spell it, and there are differences of
opinion) means to me this poem and the great wave that, in
the reign of Graul, son of Graul, broke through Crebawethan
and swept north and west. When the next dawn broke, the
kingdom had vanished. " Forest and pasture, city, mart and
haven—away to the horizon a heaving sea covered all. Of
[Graul's] kingdom there remained only a thin strip of coast,
marching beside the Cornish border, and this sentinel rock,
standing as it stands to-day, then called Cara Clowz, and now
St. Michael's Mount."*

So to the north coast and its leagues of marbled surf. This,
in modern verse, is the Betjeman country. He is a freeman of
Polzeath, master of Trebetherick, lord of St. Enodoc. We
know him for our own when he writes such lines as these :

> *Where deep cliffs loom enormous, where cascade*
> *Mesembryanthemum and stone-crop down,*
> *Where seagulls look no larger than a lark*
> *Hung midway twixt the cliff-top and the sand,*
> *Sun-shadowed valleys roll along the sea.*

On to Tintagel, to-day better imagined in Arthurian mood
than visited in mid-season, and to the little world of the elegiac
poems Hardy wrote in the spring of 1913, when Beeny, the

*Phoebus on Halzaphron. See Q's The Laird's Luck. (Dent : Duchy edition.)

Valency, St. Juliot, and the places of his courtship appeared to him in the light of fifty years before. Muriel Hawkey has chosen the finest of these moving poems :

> *I found her out there*
> *On a slope few see*
> *That falls awkwardly*
> *To the salt-edged air,*
> *Where the ocean breaks*
> *On the purple strand,*
> *And the hurricane shakes*
> *The solid land.*

Farther north Robert Stephen Hawker strides into the book in his hip-length waders, claret-hued clerical coat, and blue jersey. We go not to the "Sangraal" (dedicated so affectingly*), but to "Trelawny," of course, and to the galloping measure of the Gate-song of Stowe : "And the King and Sir Bevill for ever." Inland, there is C. E. Vulliamy to champion the Cornish moors, "infinitely more mysterious, more varied in form and mood than their neighbours."

This is inland Cornwall. I was bred by the sea : daily I opened my eyes upon "the tawny lion-guards of Kynance Cove" and on what I hold still to be one of the noblest seascapes on the British coast. But I knew also, as Muriel Hawkey did, the lonely plateau-downs of Goonhilly, "where sweet *erica* lifts her head" (Mitchell again) and the wind used to sting about Dry Tree. Later I came to the wide and deserted Bodmin Moor, that shaggy carpet hurled across the granite of the north. Bodmin Moor has not been defaced. Indeed it is wrong to speak of Cornwall, as its critics do, as only a coast-line looped about a dull emptiness. There are few lovelier and less "developed" villages than two within reach of Bodmin's "grey, shut-in street," as Betjeman calls it. Nobody who has gone out from Lostwithiel, or explored the East Cornwall villages between Liskeard, Looe, and Fowey, or roamed around Caradon, or penetrated the

---

* "To a Vacant Chair : and an Added Stone : I chant these Solitary Sounds."

Roseland, or discovered the riparian sisters of Meneage, is likely to talk for a moment of the dullness of the Cornish inland scene. The legend derives, no doubt, from a fortnight-at-Newquay tourist, a mayfly golfer, or the follow-my-leader guide-book men who never went to see for themselves. (Naturally I except such informed writers as J. W. Lambert and the late J. R. A. Hockin.) I do not forget the industrial areas. A. L. Rowse—some of his poems are here—has described memorably that queer and exciting White Country where the sand-burrows raise their cones in a mock-Alpine world. And there should be some salute for the Mining Division and the rust-peeling landscapes about Carn Brea.

This book is starred with the right names. Carew shines genially from the past. From our own century we have passages from Tregarthen, the rhythms of Q. (both " Helford " and—an interesting choice—a late poem, " The Lighthouse Seat "), Lady Vyvyan's gentle prose, poems by Frances Bellerby, Anne Treneer, Geoffrey Grigson. And Muriel Hawkey has wisely summoned Walter de la Mare and those poems of his—Cornish in spirit—that sigh and shine and glimmer, or to the moon in wavering morrice move. Some names are missing : Celia Fiennes, Polwhele, Charles Henderson—greatest of Cornish historians—Hamilton Jenkin, Charles Lee. But your anthology is the most personal of books. It is the easiest thing in the world to shoot at it, and to ask why this and that are not included. An anthologist must close eyes and ears on all but his own wishes. What Muriel Hawkey has done, and admirably, has been to choose those passages—and especially poems—that flash up for her at once the Cornwall she understands and loves. What would I have added ? Possibly one of Masefield's best lines (from the sunset of " The Begetting of Arthur "),

Tintagel blackened like a dragon's comb,
or Drinkwater's Cornish folly :
Isolt and Mark and Lancelot,
Majestical of sound,
In babble-mouth were clean forgot—
Lostwithiel is found . . .

or a few lines from Roden Noel's " Fowey." But why a second anthology? There is enough here. There are traditional songs ; there are poems by new writers (always good to find) ; there is such recent work as Margaret Willy's endearing " Child by the Harbour " from the *West Country Magazine ;* and we have poem upon poem that prove the anthologist's affection for Cornish names, as in

> *all about St. Levan and Penberth*
> *On to Pedn-Men-an-Mere,*

or in Stubbs's " Cornish Bells," the carol that has rung through the county

> *From Launceston town to Michael's Mount, from Bude to*
> *Sennen sand,*

in the nonsense-rhyme of Davies Gilbert, or in the romping ballad :

> *There were Lanlivery men, St. Mabyn men,*
> *St. Tudy and St. Kew—*
> *But the five lads of Egloshayle*
> *Did all the rest outdo.*

Finally, there is a blithe absence of piskie-poems, the whimsy and the wuthering. Nostalgia from the exiles, yes ; but that was to be expected. And what, after all, is wrong with the honestly sentimental? We are weary of the day's arrogant toughness, of sour, thin-lipped cynicism. We have far too many superior persons who seem never to have had a home. Regional loyalty is a fine thing. It is wise not to sneer at it.

A last word. Expressed in this book—and let me mix all together—is the Cornwall we know : the Cornwall of the sea-holly and the samphire, the vernal squill and the mesembryanthemum : the banners of weed, the salt in the air, the primrose, thrift, and campion, wings flashing in the sun, seals asleep, the fuchsias' dazzling arras, gulls behind the share, grey stone, glittering mica, a fisherman's trawl, mine-fingers against the blue, the deep, tangled valleys, the sand-burrows, hilly fields and stunted elms, the eager present and the overwhelming sense of the past. Cornwall, proud and independent still, is not to be patronised loftily or carelessly exploited : it remains a land apart.

When I think of it I see two pictures. First, a white beach where the rocks glisten with wet colour. Weed is plaited silkily over serpentine and sand and the flaking edge of a pigeon's-breast sea that darkens into the blue of a September night. It is time to go home, and I run—" Ben Ma Brea " under my arm—to the boulders and the sinuous cliff-face path. Behind is the steady swing of the tide. The second picture is, simply, of the battlements of Rowtor and Brown Willy piled above the moor, and of shadows rippling over the slopes beneath St. Breward. The " light and sound and darkness of the sea ": the moor's harsh splendour : those, for me, are Cornwall and home. In Muriel Hawkey's book every exile is safe at home again. On their behalf let me thank her now.

1948.   J. C. TREWIN

There's a song from the earth upspringin'
    To the music of hammer an' drill ;
'Tis sung by the wheals an' quarries
    An' streams where the claypits fill.
St. Austell an' Camborne know it,
    Delabole, Lank, Penryn ;
'Tis the song of the clay an' granite,
    Copper an slate an' tin.

There's a song from the sea upspringin'
    To the music of sails an' sheets ;
'Tis sung in the ports an' harbours
    An' fishy old twisty streets.
Padstow an' Newlyn know it,
    An' lil' ports call to the great,
The song of the pilchard an' herrin',
    Halibut, conger, an' skate.

There's a song from the fields upspringin',
    To the music of harrow an' hoe ;
'Tis glad with the hope of harvest
    When the west wind bugles blow.
Calstock an' Callington know it,
    It rolls to Whitsand Bay,
'Tis the song of the wheat an' barley,
    Clover an' oats an' hay.

The music fits together
    As the songs roll up an' down,
An' 'tis makin' a Cornish Chorus
    From Cawsand to Sennen Town ;
It rises from port and harbour,
    By Tre an' Pol an' Pen,
An' the Cornish skies are ringin'
    With the Chorus of Cornishmen.

                                BERNARD MOORE.

" THESE things remain.   Memories of sights once seen,
And faith that what has been shall be again,
And gorse and heather bloom again for me,
And bracken flame above the Cornish Sea."

A. H. GIRDLESTONE.

THE sea laments
The livelong day,
Fringing its waste of sand ;
Cries back the wind from the whispering shore—
No words I understand ;
Yet echoes in my heart a voice,
As far, as near, as these—
The wind that weeps,
The solemn surge
Of strange and lonely seas.

WALTER DE LA MARE.
Echoes

WHEN I set out for Lyonnesse
A hundred miles away
    The rime was on the spray,
And starlight lit my lonesomeness
When I set out for Lyonnesse
    A hundred miles away.

What should bechance at Lyonnesse
While I should sojourn there
    No prophet durst declare,
Nor did the wisest wizard guess
What would bechance at Lyonnesse
    While I should sojourn there.

When I came back from Lyonnesse
With magic in my eyes,
    All marked with mute surprise,
My radiance rare and fathomless,
When I came back from Lyonnesse
With magic in my eyes.

THOMAS HARDY.
When I set out for Lyonnesse

I did not know them, but their home I knew
Where lilies glimmered and the aspens grew ;
See there—beyond the farthest oakwood ride—
The flashing heron on the falling tide.

I did not know them, but I knew their gate—
Those rusted hinges—and that path of slate,
That surf of fierce, slow ivy : from the lane
Watch now the sunset in the sunken pane.

I did not know them, but I knew their sea,
That pelting flourish by the granite quay ;
Their pocket-parlour : why, she's hanging yet,
The China clipper in full canvas set.

I did not know them, but in me they live,
Eager and timid, staid and splenitive :
Their sailor's surging and their yeoman's cares—
I did not know them, yet they know me theirs.

Three lonely roofs were these, and far from mine
Where sharp spray tingles and the wet cliffs shine ;
But those, my forbears, hold the land in fee :
In them all Cornwall dwells. They dwell in me.

J. C. TREWIN.
Heritage

HERE time's robber feet have played truant, his hour-hand is
    stilled,
Merging Past in To Be on these rocks on the rim of the world
Where the white gulls lament, dipping wings that flash
    sunlight-on-snow
In the blue waste where sky melts in sea and the foam is
    uncurled.

Slow-lulled in my dreaming, I hear all the hourless day
The far, lazy lap of the waves on this lonely strand ;
Smell the salt of the surf, feel the sun warm my spread-eagled
    limbs,
And the sea-licked stones burning under my careless hand

Till I am the sparkle, the sun on the surge of the sea,
One with the dance and the dazzle, the cool swirl and swing,
And life flows as full and as free as the deep-running tide,
While thought flies in the white wheel and whirr of the swift,
    flashing wing.

MARGARET WILLY.
Sea Song

" IT bordereth on the East with *Devon* divided therefrom, in most places, by the ryver *Tamer,* which springeth neere the North Sea, at *Hartland* in *Devon,* runneth thorow *Plymouth Haven,* into the South. For the rest, the maine Ocean sundreth the same, on the North from *Ireland,* on the West from the Ilands of *Scilley,* and on the South from little *Britaine.* These borders now thus straightened, did once extend so wide, as that they enabled their inclosed territorie, with the title of a Kingdome. *Polidore Virgil* allotteth it the fourth part of the whole Iland, and the ancient Chronicles report, that *Brute* landed at *Totnes* in *Cornwall,* a Towne now seated in the midst of Devon. Moreover, until *Athelstanes* time, the *Cornish-men* bare equal sway in *Excester* with the *English* : for hee it was who hemmed them within their present limits. Lastly, the encroaching Sea hath ravined from it, the whole Countrie of Lionnesse, together with divers other parcels of no little circuite : and that such a Liennesse there was, these proofes are yet remaining. The space betweene the lands end, and the Iles of *Scilley,* being about thirtie miles, to this day retaineth that name, in Cornish *Lethowfow,* and carrieth continually an equall depth of fortie or fixtie fathom, (a thing not usual in the Seas proper Dominion) save that about the midway there lieth a Rocke, which at low water discovereth his head. They terme it the Gulfe, suiting thereby the other name of Scilla. Fishermen also casting their hooks thereabouts, have drawn up peeces of doores and windowes. Moreover, the ancient name of Saint *Michaels Mount,* was *Caraclowse* in *Cowse,* in English, *The hoare Rocke in the Wood* and which now is at evrie floud encompassed by the Sea, and yet at some low ebbes, rootes of mightie trees are discryed in the sands about it."

From *The Survey of Cornwall*
Written by RICHARD CAREW OF ANTONIE, 1602

CORNUBIA, hail ! thou land of mist and cloud,
  Along whose coasts the hurrying tempests blow
Their deep-mouthed trumpets, while, like warriors proud,
  On mighty rocks, the billows charging go.

Land of the granite peak, so wild, so bare,
Great Nature looks a ragged beggar there ;
Yet, stored beneath thy soil, rich coffers lie,
And wealth untold those dreary vaults supply.

Despite thy gloom and storms, oft smiles most bright
  Flash on thy shores from sunniest, bluest skies ;
Peace after passion, after darkness light,
  And after tears, sweet Beauty's laughing eyes.

The rainbow sits in glory on thy hills,
With dewy wine her bowl the kingcup fills ;
Soft airs blow fragrance from the daisied vale,
Where brooks sing lyrics to the throstle's tale.

O yes, the wild Land's End, Tintagel's rocks,
  May war for ever with the sounding deep ;
Granite-ribbed mountains brave the tempest's shocks,
  And the drear Mines in long, long deserts sweep ;

Yet nooks adorn rough Cornwall, sweet and blest—
So gems will grace the dusky Ethiop's breast—
Plains where fertility each blessing showers,
Glens where Arcadia smiles in fruits and flowers.

Behold bright Tamar, England's Arno, sparkling
  By groves and meads, by rocks with moss embrown'd ;
See Fowey crystal-trailing, flashing, darkling,
  While Lynher dances on with joyous bound :

Clear-bosomed Fal divides the winding steeps,
Woods fringe its course, the church-tower mirror'd sleeps ;
Beauty in greenest coves doth laughing hide,
Peace, like an angel, watching by its tide.

With glittering rocks the Lizard breasts the waves,
  Emerald and flame, beyond art's painting grand !*
Sure sea-nymphs fashioned Kynance' wondrous caves,
  Roofed with rich glory by their cunning hand.

Mount of St. Michael ! did that hallowed steep
Drop from some lovelier star, to grace our deep ?
So strange, so beautiful, it seems to stand,
Half in the clasping ocean, half on land.**

Cornwall, no more the barbarous wrecker hails
  The stranded ship, and plies his robber-trade ;
But honesty and kindness walk thy vales,
  And art and science there bright homes have made.

Proud, loyal are thy sons, and many a name
Sheds on thy cairn-crowned hills the light of fame ;
Davy and Opie, stars unfading, shine,
And while they flash their lustre, heighten thine.

NICHOLAS MICHELL.

Address to Cornwall

---

* The beautiful stone, called Serpentine, abounds at the Lizard Point—a stone, for the most part, of a deep green colour, veined with scarlet. Kynance Cove, in the neighbourhood, is considered one of the most extraordinary spots on our western coasts. Here also the rocks are composed of the rare and gorgeous marble above named.

** St. Michael's Mount, near Penzance, renowned in early religious history, is separated from the mainland twice a day by the flowing of the tide. The famous rock-pyramid of nature's formation, rising to the height of more than 200 feet, and crowned with its ancient monastic building, presents in itself a strikingly picturesque object ; while the surrounding scenery possesses a beauty and a magnificence, that cannot fail to captivate the imagination.

WORLD of the yellow gorse, and purple lea,
With fruitful ocean sounding in the caves,
Rich-veined of earth, whose ever-rolling waves
Of harvest ripen on from sea to sea ;
Thy wells have power, there saints have bent the knee,
Awe guards thy cromlechs, haunts thy moorland graves,
And at the crossway, with the sign that saves,
Hangs Balder-Christ upon his granite tree.

Still on thy greens the fairies dance their round,
The brownies haunt the hearth and clot the cream,
Tregeagle cries, the wish-hounds chase and chime ;
Thy cairns with clash of phantom arms resound,
And nights of vision melt to days of dream
Filled with romance of old Arthurian time.

H. D. RAWNSLEY.
Cornwall

THIS pool, this quiet sky
Is rippled with a chime,
Night gathers, and the cry
Of lambs in the far fold
Comes to us as we climb :
The moorland air is cold.

Ghost-pale the grass, and bare
The boulder-scattered crest.
A frightened rabbit starts—
With quickening eyes and hearts
We turn about and stare
Into the open West.

The Cornish hills lie small,
So huge the sky has grown.
We can look down on all
Western and Southern ground,
And see the Eddystone,
Pricking the seaward pall,
Wink over Plymouth Sound.

Below us, dim and deep,
Mist-hidden, murmuring,
The valley winds away :
Beneath its shadow Spring
Lies light asleep
In dreams of coming day,
With cuckoos on the wing
And steep banks blossoming.

Again the quiet sky
Is troubled with a chime
That spreads in rings of sound.
We sigh, and think, What rhyme
That man has ever bound
Can hold a sigh.

L. A. G. STRONG.
March Evening

" PELEA era why moaz, moz fettow teag,
    Gen agaz bedgeth gwin, ha agaz blew mellyn ?"
" Mi a moaz than venton, sarra wheag,
    Rag delkiow sevi gwra muzi teag."

" Pea ve moaz gen a why, moz fettow teag,
    Gen agaz bedgeth gwin, ha agaz blew mellyn ?"
" Grea mena why, sarra wheag,
    Rag delkiow sevi gwra muzi teag."

" PRAY, whither so trippingly, pretty fair maid,
  With your face rosy white, and your soft yellow
    hair?"
" Sweet Sir, to the well in the summer wood shade,
    summer wood shade,
    summer wood shade,
  For strawberry leaves make the young maiden
    fair."

" Shall I go with you, pretty fair maid, to the wood,
  With your face rosy white, and your soft yellow
    hair ?
" Sweet Sir, if you please, it will do my heart good,
    do my heart good,
    do my heart good,
  For strawberry leaves make the young maiden
    fair."

      TRADITIONAL
      Pray, Whither so Trippingly ?

Cornish words from Pryce's Archaelogia Cornu-Britannica, 1790.
English words from Worth's West Country Garland, 1875.
Tune : " Where are you going my Pretty Maid ? "

    From *Cornish Dialect and Folk Songs*

   Low in the valley's cup
    Brimmed by green hills,
   Where the shining Tamar
    Winds as it wills,

   In a hushed garden
    Memories unfold,
   Stands a stone cottage
    Growing gently old.

Autumn's leaves rustle
   At the wind's will
Like restless sleepers
   Too weary to be still.

In the blurred distance
   White sails shine,
Yes ! I hear you calling,
   Dear home of mine !

MARY VOSPER PRIOR.
Woodlands Old

God's Garden ! Well you named the spot
My childhood's Heaven unforgot ;
My eager eyes watched Spring by Spring
The wonder of its burgeoning.

There snowdrops and the bluebells ring
Their bells to usher in the Spring,
And hid within the hedges' gloom
The primrose trembles into bloom.

The sweet narcissus' stately pride
Makes holier the Eastertide,
And gusty March her bounty spills
In golden rain of daffodils.

Gay tulips marching row on row
Perpetual rainbows, brightly glow,
Shy valley lilies censers swing
To gaudy wallflowers rioting.

The bright green lawns with daisies spread,
Fruit blossoms waving overhead,
And peonies with banners gay
Swing spring-time glory into May.

Still to my heart it solace brings
Remembering other happier Springs,
And to my exiled eyes afar
Its beauty beckons like a star.

God's Garden ! Well you named the spot,
My childhood's Heaven unforgot.

MARY VOSPER PRIOR.
Spring in God's Garden
(*St. Dominic, Cornwall*)

" THE buildings are ancient, large, strong and faire, appurtenanced with the necessaries of wood, water, fishing, parks, and mils, with the devotion of (in times past) a rich furnished Chappell, and with the charity of almes-houses for certain poore people whom the owners used to releeve. It is reported and credited thereabouts, how Sir Richard Edgcumb the elder was driven to hide himself in those his thick woods, which overlook the river, what time being suspected of favoring the Earl of Richmond's party, against King R. the 3. hee was hotly pursued, and narrowly searched for. Which extremity taught him a sudden policy, to put a stone in his cap, and tumble the same into the water, while these rangers were fast at his heeles, who looking down after the noyse, and seeing his cap swimming thereon, supposed that he had desperately drowned himself, gave over their further hunting, and left him liberty to shift away, and slip over into Brittaine : for a grateful remembrance of which delivery, hee afterwards builded in the place of his lurking, a Chappell not yet utterly destroyed."

RICHARD CAREW.
Cuttayle
(*Cotehele*)
From *Survey of Cornwall*, 1602.

WHERE between leafy uplands glides
The Tamar with her changing tides,
Kissing the shores of either shire,
Until she meets her Ocean sire,
There, high above the girdling wood,
Cotehele's quaint mansion long has stood ;
Just as it is, four centuries past
It look'd, and will as many last.

Firm stands its grey embattled wall,
The rusted armour crowds the hall,
And the queer carven furniture
Doth still the worm's slow tooth endure :
The storied tapestry still hangs,
Scarce injured by the moths' keen fangs ;
And on the stout limb'd board remain
The cups our fathers loved to drain.

H. SEWELL STOKES.
From " *Cotehele*." *1871.*

IN that deep, quiet valley there is peace.
The stream beside the old grey mill provides
The only swiftly-flowing turbulence.
On all sides of the valley Nature's tides
In season ebb and flow.   The earth's increase
Each year is gathered under the warm glow
Of Summer's sun.   In Winter, under snow
New life's begun, and seeds begin to swell
Ready for wakening, when through the earth
The shoots of green, and breaking buds will tell
That Spring is here in place of Winter's dearth.
Soon swelling buds on all the orchard trees
Give promise of the Summer's succulence.
And Primroses will scent the woodland breeze
And Bluebells spread a shimmering haze along
The path, where Beech and Oak and Chestnut grow

With lacy light through leaves, and trunks grown strong
With age. And from the path we see below
The Tamar flowing out to meet the Sound.
Here it is tidal, and a faint sea-smell
Is mingled with the scents of flowers around.
And here the little Chapel stands, to tell
From long ago, of one man's gratitude
For sanctuary on this fair estate.
And listening to the evening song of birds
With thankfulness we too commemorate
Our joy and peace, in song of written words.

LORNA L. HAWKEY.
Cotehele Valley

I.

HERE once more is the brilliant confusion of summer !
I had not thought to behold again
The buttercups, and the tall red luminous sorrel,
The wiry-stalked grasses shaking the light in their flowers,
And the kingly host of foxgloves in purple splendour
Down the quarry slope
At the wood's edge.

Here once more is the wind-flung motley of fragrance !
I had not thought to smell again
These thousand flowers—hawthorn—mountain ash,
Sun-battered water and stone and timber and earth ;
Green-ness ; and faint over meadow and woodland and moor,
Tangy, elusive,
The summer sea.

Here once more is the exquisite disorder of birdsong !
I had not thought to hear again
The countless cuckoo-game of cup-and-ball
At the first glint of dawn, and then the spreading
Out, like a fan, of the vast orchestra ;
Anarchist singers
In heedless accord.

2.

Now butterflies dance ; and dances the light
Like a tree-netted shoal of fish
High over the cottage roof
In the tossing foliage.

Now flutter, unsettled, the wings of light,
Hesitant, wavering, delicate,
Over the deep orchard grass
And the moss-yellow bark of the trees.

Now from the chestnut horse glows burning light,
The fly on the leaf is a jewel,
The thistledown hair of the child
A pale torch at the cottage door.

3.

Oh, here once more is the tearing anguish of sorrow,
The bitterness !
I had not thought to prepare again for departure,
Cry another Hail and Farewell ; for all was accomplished ;
The agony past, away had I turned, quiet-footed,
And should before now
Have gone very far.

FRANCES BELLERBY
Departure Postponed

I heard those voices to-day again :
Voices of women and children, down in that hollow
Of blazing light into which swoops the tree-darkened lane
Before it mounts up into the shadow again.

I turned the bend—just as always before
There was no one at all down there in the sunlit hollow ;
Only ferns in the wall, foxgloves by the hanging door
Of that blind old desolate cottage.   And just as before

I noticed the leaping glitter of light
Where the stream runs under the lane ; in that mine-dark
        archway
—Water and stones unseen as though in the gloom of night—
Like glittering fish slithers and leaps the light.

I waited long at the end of the lane,
But heard only the murmuring water under the archway.
Yet I tell you, I've been to that place again and again,
And always, in summer weather, those voices are plain,
Down near that broken house, just where the tree-darkened
        lane
Swoops into the hollow of light before mounting to shadow
        again . . . .

                                FRANCES BELLERBY
                                Voices

        ABOVE the endless sighing of the sea
        Old songs are tossed into the gentle night,
        The soft-voiced singers leaning on the wall
        Where sang and watched their fathers.
                        No least change
        Senses the innocent sea, but the same loved songs
        In the same soft lilting voices as of old.
        Fathers or sons, where is the difference ?
        For all is endless to the sighing sea.

Listening blind with tears,
Am I wiser than the sea ?
In every song is silence,
In every meeting, parting,
And in all love, bereavement,
And in every birth is death.
And soon, soon, all is over
Save the sighing of the sea.

FRANCES BELLERBY.
The Innocence of the Sea

". . . CORNWALL is a land of echoes. It is full of hidden places
where dwell the memories of bygone days, full of creeks and
coves and valleys where many a haunting presence lingers.

Some of us it may be, have seen strange little men no higher
than a span, little grey men at play among the grasses or the
moonbeams ; seen tiny greyish gnomes perched a-swinging on
the thistle seed ; or been aware of shadowy figures peering
in the woodland, figures with a frozen smile and long arms
waving, faces lurking, for good or evil, in the leafage in
between each twisted branch.

Or we have heard, in some unrippled creek at dead of
night, the wailing of one doomed to everlasting sorrow. We
have listened to the whistling of the wind in some old
chimney-stack among the mines, where the owls hoot and
scream in sole possession ; to the sighing of the wind among
the sand-hills, with that strangest of all sounds between earth
and heaven, the hollow echo of a sigh. We have heard the
booming of the breakers in many a subterranean cave, the
long, reverberating boom that shakes the earth to its founda-
tions ; the sound, half threatening, half triumphant, of those
breakers for ever dashing on the rocks, and for ever sucking
back into the deep to gather for a new attack.

In Cornwall there is many a half-heard whisper, many a
sound and fleeting presence that can never be explained.

Deep in the woodland that is mirrored in one winding river, there is a promontory lonely as the dawn ; it runs out towards the middle of the river, a shadowed house stands there among the trees, a shadowed house without a neighbour, and spindle-wood and briers grow to the very door. Whoever will listen from that house at midnight may hear strange music on the quiet reaches of the water, a sound of oars that were never made by human hand, of voices that fell silent very long ago. Then, swiftly, that Phoenician galley will pass up with the flowing tide ; the splash of oars, the sound of foreign voices will die away among the oak trees on the farther shore, and the silence of the night will swallow up those memories.

In another lonely parish there are hanging woods above a valley, and the village lies beside a stream where it is widened to a marsh. Long ago, before the valley was silted up with washings from the tin mines, many a ship would glide between the hanging woods. Many a night-run cargo was landed on the quay that crumbles now above the marsh, many a strange sea-oath rang out in the little inn beside the stream. The fiddler came across the water, the country folk from far and near rode in to the village tavern. At that time there were sounds of revelry by day and night, with never any thought, restraint nor kindness, and the three most wicked women in the country had their dwelling there.

But now there are no sounds of merriment, and brambles intertwine across the track where once the mules filed up and down with burdens. The memory of those days is yet alive in the very stones, the earth, the atmosphere ; it lurks among the reed-beds in the valley. That is why unearthly sounds ring out in the stillness of the night, wailing of souls that never reach a haven, a clamour of strange wickedness ; and then, like the tolling of some bell, a heavy sense of doom and sorrow.

The place is haunted with these memories and sounds, and hardly is that man or woman who will venture out alone to listen to the wailing in the darkness ; for there is power in that wailing, power of some evil thing about to seize its prey.

The sun will rise and set, the moon will wax and wane, and still the memories gather.

Red-faced, hurrying, the tourist of to-day will rest his knapsack by the old grey stones, will bare his head to the sunshine and, standing there in the silence, will muse awhile on things that are, and things that have been, and things that never were. For, in this land of echoes, through all the ages men have felt a sense of something great, of something other than their little lives, of something calling, calling, with an urgency above entreaty or command ; and memories of God and thoughts of worship have ever been like a living presence.

*   *   *

But it is not only with the fairy men and mermaids that these echoes are concerned, nor with thoughts of crime and sacrifice and ghostly music heard by mortal ear ; nor indeed with any sound that was caught and given back again in space, any sound that will gather in the valley and roll among the hills, only to lose itself between earth and sky.

It is rather with the little memories of familiar things, memories of a well-remembered time, that come pealing down the years like a chime from far away ; rather with that sudden lifting of the veil, when, in some weary humdrum life, eyes look upward for one moment and have ' glimpses that would make me less forlorn,' when ears will catch some echoes from a spirit-world.

Very soon . . . these memories will be forgotten. The very words, those old, expressive Cornish words, no longer will be heard, no longer understood. Surely it is well to gather up the memories while we may . . . .

Yes, Cornwall is a land of echoes ; spirit echoes ; echoes of the past ; and we, if we are fain to hear, must listen low and reverently. We shall not meet romance on every brier-bush and high road, nor feel the throb of Celtic passion behind each face of working man and woman, beneath the tones of every day. Only, now and then, between the lights, from carn and cliff and boulder, there will rise a little whisper telling of those immemorial secrets hidden in the heart of stone and water ; and then, with the coming of darkness, all is still and hidden once again. Only there will come, it may be soon, it may be late, a look on hardened faces, perhaps the sudden lifting of an eyebrow, the breaking of a tight-lipped silence, and there will be an echo from a spirit world, some light thrown upward for a moment from a leaping flame of thought and feeling.

Those who seek display of Celtic fire in all the little ways of daily life will seek and ever seek again ; but always just behind the old grey rocks, beyond the mist of the moorland, beneath the silence of the Cornishman, there lurks a sense of deep things seen and felt and well remembered, of beauty burning like a flame, of mystery that colours all the land."

C. C. ROGERS.

From *Echoes in Cornwall*

In the holy well tucked into the green hill
The yellow wings of the moths, dead souls
Of the dead, lie on the still pool.

A bent pin perhaps will bring your wish but
Is this still a centre of mysteries, or
A holy place, of the mother of David ?

In the rotting bearded alders below grow
The Royal fern, and the mallard collects there
Its blue sad eggs in the warm down,

The lean salmon slides through the pools ;
And in the farm the pathway is closed,
And they breed foxes for their silver coats in pens.

Forgotten above the well, behind the island of oaks,
The uneven ground and the ragwort and the brambles
Over the stumps of the chapel, where

They prayed for the black souls of those who believed
In God, in the mother of God and the mother of David ;
And then the bell called

More clearly in the valley, than now these wild ducks
And the fern and the young red of the oaks ; though sold
In the twisted ink, all, all

Forgotten. Still this holy well persists, which
Forewent them, and the yellow wings float
On the round water ; and the guide book

Declares there are Maltese crosses circling the granite
Rim : liverworts now conceal them.
And the legend, how the farmer who bought

The bells, removed the basin with oxen, and the chain
Snapped and the basin rolled back to its cell
Which God commanded it ? The cottages

About, of mud mixed with straw, are in ruins,
The death, copulation, and birth under their flaked
Whitewash are of woodlice and spiders :

The limekiln is choked and the wet lead mines
Chuckle to the stone of water, the ravens nest
In the mine-house, the buzzard spirals

Over the red oaks, the woodpeckers whinney
And the polished adder in the deserted orchard coils
By the orpine : " Live Long " they call it.

Herodsfoot, Coldrennick, Plashtown,
Yearls Coombe, Keglenna,—they are not incidents even
On the straight road of the screaming dipper,

They are unknown to the jerking sand-piper, the red and black
Warrior ants piling their stick nest in the hedge,
The tabby gone wild, hunting

Under the bracken. Stir the still wings
And wish—wish for what? Would you be the suave adder
Or the exhausted salmon slipping back to the sea?

Be the spiralling buzzard, or the near dipper,
Or lichen bearding the alder? Or else the river
Smoothing the quartz in its unfeeling,

Folding eternity? Do you envy the other ages?
Of the well and the souls, the bell, the incense, the predatory
Men or the solid progression of farmers?

Envy the clack and clink of the mines,
The fumes of the limekiln, the islanded heron,
Or otter, or orpine, or the spider and louse?

O in the wild tropic of this valley, give up no will
For wish. In its deadly life, still, still,
Although the foreign foxes whine

And the hunt horns and shrieks for the otter, under
The willowed dumps of the mine glitter
The fierce oddments of silver and still

Lies black and pure, unworried, holding the wings
Of yellow, this round, perverted symbol, past
The mud and scramble, of our own will.

GEOFFREY GRIGSON.
The Well in the Valley

OVER the harbour
The restless seabirds
Clamour and whirl
In the glow of the morning,
Swooping in flocks
To the cool clear water,
Where fishers are hauling
Their catch to the quayside.
Keen are the airs
That rise from the sea-way,
Merged with the magical
Breathings of summer,
Scent of the grasses,
The bushes, the blossom—
Here where I linger
With thrill and with wonder.
Then through the narrow
And tortuous byways,
Over the cobbles
I pass, by the doorways,
Quick with the stirring
Of life—see the children,
Ruddy from sleep
As they wend to the school-house ;
Down to the bridge
By the chattering rivulet,
Where fisher-wives gather
With pitchers for water.
Loudly the gulls cry,
Wheeling in flashes,
Poising in dozens
On chimney and housetop ;
Then rousing again
In a network of whiteness,
Weaving and circling,
They clamour incessant ;
While the men at the quayside

Are busily weighing
The mackerel, the ray,
The slippery congers.
Dreaming, I watch,
While my thoughts like the seabirds
Cleave to the water
Or soar to the sunlight ;
Tranced with the love
Of these beautiful seabirds,
Love of the fishers,
The vessels, the homeside ;
Staying to gaze,
That the magic impression
May live in remembrance
For nurture and solace,
In the slow seasons
Of exile that wait me.

ARTHUR L. SALMON.
Seagulls at Polperro

A WOMAN SPEAKS

HERE from the Lighthouse garden seat
    I watch the steamers trailing West ;
Almost I hear their engines beat
    And take their pulsing to my breast.

So still the evening silken-spread !
    So soft the twilit Channel heaves !
As soft the lantern overhead
    In skeins of light its warning weaves.

It warned my Sailor of the rocks
    To sea, to seas beyond again . . .
To-night the homing birds in flocks
    Will slay their life against its pane !

And I—ah, selfish—I shall rise
　And lift and drop each broken neck ;
As shutters their sea searching eyes
　Closed, closed to take of ship or wreck !

The trawlers off the Eddystone
　Have lit their lights and sunk their nets :
Through shells and dread disorder strown
　They dredge a floor for my regrets.

They dredge a floor of dream that was
　A floor two lovers danced upon :
But never fetch that shoe of glass
　My Prince had found and fitted on.

O gentle Jesu, is it Sin
　To bring to Thee my fairy tale ?
O Helper once that hushed the din
　And still'd off Galilee the gale !

A land-wind faints upon the Sea,
　A sob from far behind the hill—
" Gethsemane ! Gethsemane !"
　'Tis the Sea answers, " Peace be still."

　　　　　　　SIR A. T. QUILLER-COUCH.
　　　　　　　The Lighthouse Seat

" THE town and river of Fowey . . . lie so deeply in the valley
that nothing is seen of either till the road has merged upon
an open hillside almost overhanging the convolutions of the
estuary ; and the suddenness with which this view discloses
itself adds immensely to the effect. One moment there is
nothing to be seen but the windings of an unlovely road.
The next there has opened far below a dark green highway,
broad and spacious, branching among hills. Deep down at
the foot of the descent lie the roofs and cottages of Bodinnick,
with its heavy ferry boat lumbering across to Fowey, of which

quaint hillside town more and more is seen at every winding
of the road, till at length one's sight is drawn off it by the
disclosure of that noble view which roused old Carew to
eloquence nearly four centuries ago, and which still remains
an unforgettable memory with those who have seenit. ' In
passing along,' says the squire of Antony, ' your eyes shall
be called away from guarding your feet to descry by their
furthest kenning the vast ocean, sparkled with ships, that
continually this way trade forth and back to most quarters
of the world. Nearer home they take view of all sized cocks,
barges and fisher boats hovering on the coast. Again,
contracting your sight to a narrower scope, it lighteth on the
fair and commodious haven, where the tide daily presenteth
his double service of flowing and ebbing, to carry and recarry
whatsoever the inhabitants shall be pleased to charge him
withal, and his creeks, like a young wanton lover, fold about
the land with many embracing arms.'

The salt air mingles strangely with the scent of violets
as we descend the hill, and the sweet odour of the woodlands
unites with a decided savour of tarry rope. One could drop
a pebble on the roofs of the four or five houses which stand
about the higher end of the sloping pier, pretty white-washed
cottages, of that neat aspect which sometimes enables the
Cornishman to recognise the dwellings of his own people in
other countries. For the Cornish peasant's garden is full of
stocks and roses. I know not what it is that is peculiarly
Cornish in the growth of these common flowers, or of the
valerian that flames crimson on the low walls, or the tamarisk
that surmounts it, or it may be something that I am not
observant enough to detect and isolate. But whatever it may
be, certain I am that a Cornish garden may be known far
away from Cornwall, and I myself have recognized one at
a glance in the wilds of Donegal, where the stocks and roses
bloomed as sweetly under the shadow of Muckish and Horn
Head as ever they did in Fowey or Bodmin, and the true
sense of Cornish kinship blossomed sweetly too in the heart
of an old Saltash woman who, for many a year had not heard
a Cornish tongue, and could not make enough of it when

found, but laughed and cried and chattered all at once till she brought to mind in very soberness that great passion which beset Sordello on the Mount of Purgatory, when he heard Virgil speaking in the tongue of his own city, Mantua.

I might pause here to say much of the intense feeling which the Cornish cherish for their homes and for their own wild and beautiful country, a feeling which neither years nor exile can do aught but strengthen, and which, as far as I know, has been little recognised in literature. Perhaps the reason may be that which makes me stay my pen, and refrain from writing down for other men to wonder at what is too strongly felt to be easily expressed.

The dusk has fallen while we are waiting for the ferry boat. The few vessels lying in the harbour have lit their lanterns. Across the water come the faint noises of a wheezy hurdy-gurdy, and the cries of children ; and one sees on an open spot beside the quay a tent in which some rustic tragedy is being acted. We are landed on a dark and slippery jetty, and go through the dim old town too weary to notice more than that its streets are steep and tortuous, and that through many openings and courtyards we see the dark water washing to and fro."

ARTHUR H. NORWAY.
Fowey

THE rich red of evening sun on the harrowed field,
The chittering of birds,
The insistent drone of planes out at sea,
The scolding rooks,
The colder tones of the water :
What is there in a Cornish hedge,
The broken herring-bone pattern of stones,
The gorse, the ragged rick,
The way the little elms are,
Sea-bent, sea-shorn,
That so affects the heart ?

A. L. ROWSE.
Cornish Landscape

THE whole bay brimming with the silent sea,
The call of a curlew, the creaking of a plough,
A black and satin plane slides suddenly over
Wheeling to the coast,
The smell of November in the air,
The mould, the dead brambles, the year over,
In the distance the familiar cone
Of Rame Head, so known
To Drake and Hawkins and Frobisher
And all those long-dead seafaring men
Outward bound to the Spanish Main,
Or homeward driving with a merry gale
Of Spring or Autumn centuries ago.
Yet still the coast they'd know
And find it only strange that other later men
Should claim priority in places that were theirs.

The red stain of Autumn on the upper slopes,
The noises of afternoon, trees, plane, gulls,
Rising and falling to a subdued murmur,
The vivid red of leaves, of herb robert,
The flower dead, the corrugated rocks,
Skin of rhinoceros or mastodon,
The cleft coves cloven by evening shadow,
The winterblue wind when the sun goes down,
Insinuating in the window-seams,
Makes clear and poignant the lines of the landscape
Like a picture of one's childhood, exposed, irrevocable.

A. L. ROWSE.
November Ploughing

How can one express
At once the mingled sadness
And sense of joy
In the glitter on the sea ?

The pathos and regret
That stir the heart yet
When one recalls
The cries of gulls ?

Or put into words
The leap of the heart
When a boy puts out in his boat
From the little port ?

If I could say
All that arises in me
As I look down on the bay
From this eyrie :

The childhood vision that lay
Out between sea and sky
Beyond the horizon
Which no eye could descry :

The rounded clouds that were
The heads of angels in choir,
The sky's blue vacancies
The tents of Paradise ;

The sound of water at night
Falling through the woods,
Making more solitary
The ancient solitudes :

Or stars hung over the hillside,
Snow and Christmas time,
The Blessed Virgin and Child,
The shepherds of Bethlehem.

If I understood these things
That have such power to move,
I should perhaps understand
The mystery of love :

The universe would unfold
Its secret heart to me
As a sea-flower opens and shuts
And slips into the sea.

A. L. ROWSE.
If I Could Say

THE bus goes up the valley road
  With mounds of gorse on either hand
That burn and blaze amid the brake
  And clothe with fire the hills of sand.

Sunlight on a grey stone house,
  The ivies glitter and catch the light ;
The sparse and scattered Cornish trees
  Announce Carthew, and now the white

Claypits on the pock-marked moor :
  We pass the granite cottages,
The gardens with a shrub in flower,
  The rude and honest villages,

Treverbyn, Roche and Stenalees :
  We mark across the open moor,
Sunshine and shadow on the flank,
  The rhinoceros of Helman Tor.

A lane leads to Tremodret farm—
  Name of ill omen for Arthur's kin ;
The old toll-house of Lockingate,
  The chess-board fields are brown and green.

White drifts of blackthorn fringe the road
  That winds and swerves among the hills,
The black ploughed earth, Lanivet tower,
  The gulls afloat on inland pools.

How different a countryside
  From where I seem to see you still :
The water meadows of the Stour,
  Constable's ford and Flatford Mill.

A. L. ROWSE.
Bus-ride

In the heart of Cornwall, there are so many quiet roads and bylanes which seem to begin in no particular place, and end without having served any particular purpose—unless it be to delight the heart of the solitary traveller. One such lane I know, along which I often walk alone ; it is a winding lane which threads its way along the edge of Tresillian Creek, a mile above Malpas—the traditional meeting-place of Tristan and Isolde.

There is a seat there to which I often go alone and meditate ; hushed by the wind in the pines, and soothed by the lap of little waves against the rocks at my feet, I find it easy to step inside the gates of heaven, and, without any difficulty at all to become utterly at peace with the world. My seat is formed by the tangled roots of an old oak whose branches, like all exposed trees in Cornwall, make exaggerated and dramatic gestures against the skyline. Beside me, the purple sea-asters and the tufts of pink thrift mingle with the delicate amethyst of the sunlit mud-banks. Here, looking towards Lamorran and St. Just-in-Roseland, I lean back to listen to the lamentations of innumerable curlews and the guttural cries of the gulls.

Sometimes, in Autumn, I stop on my way towards my secret eyrie to gather blackberries—for they are edible far into October—or to pluck the slate-blue sloes, whose powdery bloom is defaced at a touch. I could tell you where and when to gather wild strawberries in this lane ; I could promise to lead you to a pair of bullfinches, for they are always in a certain hedge ; or I could lead you, in April, to the lichen-domed nest of the long-tailed tit. But then, it is a joy to walk along a Cornish lane at any time of the year, whether in Spring, among the sloe-blossom and the peach-scented gorse, past the drifts of wild hyacinths, primroses and violets—or whether in Autumn, when the hedges are merry with hips and haws and alive with the 'tuck-tuck' of fieldfares and redwings. And who cannot recall with pleasure those summer mornings spent among heather and ling, at the edge of some lonely moor, where only the plaintive mewing of the soaring buzzards or the song of a meadow-pipit could be heard ?

To me, there is a magic in the changing Cornish scene, which can best be sensed inland—particularly among the wooded valleys of the Fal and Helford rivers. There is just such a magic about the Under-Road as it leaves the beautiful village of St. Clement and passes beneath the lichen-fragrant trees at the edge of the creek. On the way, one gets an occasional peep of the creek and its mud-banks, clothed right down to the water's edge with thick woodland. Half a mile beyond, the road passes a large pond upon which the alert bird-watcher may see anything from a spoonbill to a dabchick, according to the season of the year. And, when the tide is full, having the appearance of a tranquil lake, or low—so that it is a mere brook between the steep mud-banks—the ' ebbers ' will be out with their ebbing-nets, standing like lone sentinels in their boats.

If I were asked to summarize the character of the inland Cornish scene, I should do so in these simple phrases : lichen and ivy on trees—cobalt skies—silver-grey granite—white ' cob ' and thatch. It is almost impossible to find a tree in Cornwall which is not well bearded with lichen or thick with ivy. Nowhere else, surely, are the skies such a deep, mysterious blue ! And then, the tiny fragments of mica and felspar in the granite of walls and churches, produce a shimmering silveriness that must be seen to be believed.

Along the edge of Tresillian Creek, the granite wall which once kept back the invading tides has fallen into decay, so that its boulders are strewn in confusion on the little beaches, providing happy hunting grounds for the dunlin, oystercatcher and common sandpiper. Under these stones, particularly where a brook enters the creek, the small boys of the village hunt for crabs and silver-eels.

One of these fresh-water brooks enters the creek quite close to my favourite seat, and the sweet sound of its tumbling waters is music to the tired ear. And who, in these noisy days, does not occasionally suffer from a tired ear? So dulled have our ears become to the sweet music of Nature, that we seldom stop, look or listen—but hurry by, all too intent on getting somewhere or being somebody. If only men knew how to be forever at rest ! If only men knew how to listen for that still, small voice which I have so often heard, sitting as I do, alone beneath the murmurous pines at the edge of this tranquil creek !

It was here that I once caught from the cosmic the Universal sigh of humanity :

" O God of the silent pools and still, wide waters !
O God of the harvest and of the birth of things
—of acorn and violet, cloud and sunset—
hear us, and record the ache of our souls,
lest we be cast away forever from Thee
—lest we lose forever Thy dear tranquillity !"

But peace, like the Kingdom of Heaven, is in the hearts of men. As I sat alone beneath my overspreading oak, it was as though I saw n the dead leaves at my feet a symbol of an eternal truth : Not until the leaf dies can the seed be fed ; not until the stone is rolled away from the tomb which is the heart of man, can we be resurrected and made one with the life-beautiful.

As I returned along the Under-Road, I stopped for a moment and looked out across the silent creek. A lone curlew flew swiftly down the river, uttering its sad and mysterious call. Even so, I thought, my soul and I fly together over the waters of eternity—my soul and its vague reflection—sometimes apart and indistinct, but often twain and close—meeting, as it were, in time and space.

W. P. HODGKINSON.
The Under-Road

Know you Lamorran woods with bluebell hue
Still hail a bridal radiance of trees,
And trout, like blown leaf shadows, flicker through
The pools in Kennal vale, where no one sees ?
Know you that seals still sleep off West Pentire,
Slow swayed on the incessant surge and swell,
While winds from seaward temper Summer's fire ?

Watch ! and the friendly hours cast on their spell.
Know you Restronguet creek ? Still curlew call
Peoples the empty tide twixt ebb and flow.
Flood tide, then ebb ; Autumn's slow flare : leaves' fall ;
The years as silent come, and swiftly go.
Know you that all this waits, and changes not,
Or else God change, leaving his work forgot ?

PETER ROWLANDS.
Sonnet

Time has no power in this tranquil place,
Here nothing stirs save where the restless tide
Retreats, returns, changes its fickle mind,
And bares again the rocks it strove to hide.

Midstream the circling ripples slowly ebb,
Change to a green stillness, reflect, display
A passing bird, trees at the river's edge,
The quiet sky and the twilight end of day.

A.S.
The Estuary
King Harry Passage, Cornwall

THE curlew cry in lonely places
Up the river where dark trees frown
To the water's edge and little fields
Fall steeply down.

The little fields are closely grown
With low-laid pimpernel
And blue-eyed speedwell
And neat white clover
And round sea-pinks
Growing low, where winds do blow,
Close to the ground the whole hill over
In little fields that fall steeply down.

The curlew cry in lonely places,
Cool, sweet, melancholy, they cry,
Up the river where dark trees frown
To the water's edge and little fields
Fall steeply down.

JOYCE GRENFELL.
Cornish Estuary

THE large, calm harbour lies below
Long, terraced lines of circling light :
Without, the deep sea currents flow :
    And here are stars, and night.

No sight, no sound, no living stir,
But such as perfect the still bay :
So hushed it is, the voyager
    Shrinks at the thought of day.

We glide by many a lanterned mast ;
Our mournful horns blow wild to warn
Yon looming pier : the sailors cast
    Their ropes, and watch for morn.

Strange murmurs from the sleeping town,
And sudden creak of lonely oars
Crossing the water, travel down
    The roadstead, the dim shores.

A charm is on the silent bay ;
Charms of the sea, charms of the land.
Memories of open wind convey
    Peace to the harbour strand.

Far off, Saint David's crags descend
On seas of desolate storm : and far
From this pure rest, the Land's drear End,
    And ruining waters are.

LIONEL JOHNSON.
In Falmouth Harbour

I, living with delight
This rich autumnal day,
Mark the gulls' curving flight
Across the black-girt bay.

And the sea's working men,
The fisher-folk I mark
Haul down their boats, and then
Launch from the deep sea dark.

Far out the strange ships go ;
Their broad sails flashing red
As flame, or white as snow :
The ships as David said.

Winds rush and waters rol :
Their strength, their beauty brings
Unto mine heart the whole
Magnificence of things :

That men are counted worth
A part upon this sea,
A part upon this earth,
Exalts and heartens me.

LIONEL JOHNSON.
Cadgwith

HERE where the cliff rises on high
The sea below fills half the sky
And ships hang in mid-air,
Set on the cliff-face, square by square,
Walls of veronica enclose
White gladioli in their neat rows
And blue and golden irises ;
But though the walls grow tall as trees,
Some flowers from their quiet quillets pass
To mix with wayside weeds and grass,
Like nuns that from their strict retreats
Go visiting the poor in their plain streets,

ANDREW YOUNG
Cornish Flower Farm

How many miles to Mylor
  By frost and candle-light :
How long before I arrive there
  This mild December night ?

As I mounted the hill to Mylor
  Through the thick woods of Carclew,
A clock struck the three-quarters,
  And suddenly a cock crew.

At the cross-roads on the hill-top
. The snow lay on the ground,
In the thick air and the stillness
  No movement and no sound.

" How is it ?" said a voice from the bushes
   Beneath a rowan-tree ;
" Who is it ?" my mouth re-echoed,
   My heart went out of me.

I cannot tell what queerness
   There lay around Carclew :
Nor whatever stirred in the hedges
   When an owl replied " Who-whoo ?"

A lamp in a lone cottage,
   A face in a window-frame,
Above the snow a wicket,
   A house without a name.

How many miles to Mylor
   This dark December night :
And shall I ever arrive there
   By frost or candle-light ?

A. L. ROWSE.

How Many Miles to Mylor ?

HELFORD River, Helford River,
   Blessed may ye be !
We sailed up Helford River
   By Durgan from the sea.

O to hear the hawser chain
   Rattle by the ferry there !
Dear, and shall we come again
   By Bosahan,
By wood and water fair ?

All the wood to ransack,
   All the wave explore—
Moon on Calamansack,
   Ripple on the shore.

—Laid asleep and dreaming
   On our cabin beds ;
Helford River streaming
   By two happy heads ;

—Helford River, streaming
   By Durgan to the sea,
Much have we been dreaming
   Since we dreamed of thee.

Dear, and shall we dream again
   The one dream there ?
All may go if that remain
   By Bosahan,
And the old face wear !

                    SIR A. T. QUILLER-COUCH.
                    Helford River

SCREAMED the far sea-mew. On the mirroring sands
Bell-shrill the oyster-catchers. Burned the sky.
Couching my cheeks upon my sun-scorched hands,
Down from bare rock I gazed. The sea swung by

Dazzling dark blue and verdurous, quiet with snow,
Empty with loveliness, with music a-roar,
Her billowing summits heaving noon aglow—
Crashed the Atlantic on the cliff-ringed shore.

Drowsed by the tumult of that moving deep,
Sense into outer silence fainted, fled ;
And rising softly, from the fields of sleep,
Stole to my eyes a lover from the dead ;

Crying an incantation—learned, Where ? When ? . . .
White swirled the foam, a fount, a blinding gleam
Of ice-cold breast, cruel eyes, wild mouth—and then
A still dirge echoing on from dream to dream.

                    WALTER DE LA MARE.
                    Flotsam

" Who gazes on yon holy place,
Whose tower is marbled with the trace
Of centuries which have past away,
Sowing the cankers of decay . . .
On Landewednack's sacred pile,
And gives it not a passing smile ?
A smile of reverence and awe,
To think how well it stands the blow ;
To view that holy, aged state,
Which all who feel, must venerate.
But if it be the tourist's mood
To seek for a sublimer food ;
Or if from canzonel releas'd
The bard would seek a nobler feast ;
'Tis found magnificently deep,
At Kynance Cove, whose awful steep
In terror lives, and on the shore
We hear a new Charybidis' roar ;
Whose voice is as the thunder loud,
When bursting from the direful cloud,
Its wrath is hurl'd upon the land ;
And ravages on either hand,
A vast pneumatic engine wrought
By powers too great for common thought.
Or traveller . . . would you seek to see
The beetling rocks immensity ;
Mount them and cast your eyes below ;
Thrilling the strong electric blow
Which all must feel, when from such height
They gaze on depths, majestic might . . .

Though a Cimmerian darkness dwells
Upon the Lizard's moss grown dells ;
Bare of the robes which verdure gives
Spots where alone Disorder lives . . .
'Tis sweet to see the varied hue,
More chequer'd than e'en painter drew,

That decks the wild and frowning moor,
And coronets the angry shore.
There spreads the Deep unto the bound,
Where the horizon chains it round ;
Here we may view a fertile glade
And there the ivied crag's dark shade ;
Here stands a temple built for prayer,
A cottage and a garden there—
Here do we catch the streamlet's sigh,
A rapid torrent there sweeps by.
But let us on our fruitful rounds
Traverse across Goonhilly Downs ;
Where sweet Erica lifts her head,
In wildness of profusion spread ;
Rising around in truant play
Soothing the dark and dreary way,
To where Gunwalloe's aged fane,
In lonely mood, and lowly mien,
Is shadowed by the rising hill,
Where all is dreary, all is still.
No sound wakes Echo from her cave,
Saving the murmur of the wave ;
But in this waste how sweet to see,
A place to worship Deity !"

ROBERT HUNT, 1829.
From *The Mount's Bay*

THE old church stands hidden from the world, half-way down a winding lane that runs to the sea ; many miles from the railway, far from towns and traffic, at the remote end of a wild moorland peninsula. All the way down the lane the knotted trees form an arch of green leaves ; they lean awry as if they had grown now hither, now thither, at the mercy of every chance impulse and passing wind.

The grey church is one of the oldest in these parts and the irregular traceries on the porch are already smoothed by green mould. Inside there is a beautiful reading-desk and font, and the hush peculiar to old country churches. It is not the hush of emptiness but rather a full silence where the very stillness is weighted with memory.

Even more impressive than those relics of olden times are the thoughts awakened by the memorial tablets on the walls. Here are no set perfunctory valedictions to departed friends ; each inscription carries a warm remembrance of good will, of active life and lamented death. There is no hint of the stagnation that one would expect in this remote corner of the land ; a breath of the sea and of foreign parts is borne in nearly every phrase. In this little buried hamlet men have led lives that were neither wasted nor uneventful. They were all apparently soldiers or sailors or parsons. The parsons were active, many-sided, well-beloved ; the others were full of adventure and high courage.

Sitting there alone in the hush of the little grey building one feels that the walls are lined, not with dead words, but with living presences ; and as each one stands out with individual features he attains, by means of a simple inscription, some measure of that life in death which we all unconsciously desire.

Following the course of the green lane that leads to the Cove, one passes a row of cottages where all the homely occupations of the people are performed in the roadway. A lobster basket lies in the middle of the path, and a carpenter's bench where a man stands sawing a stake. There are suggestions of spring-cleaning in a carpet flung over the hand-rail that fences off the stream.

The cottage gardens are gay with white stocks and wall-flowers, tree-mallow, fuschia and climbing geraniums. Coils of rope hang on the hazels that overhang the stream ; no man-made hooks or cupboards are needed here, for Nature provides them all. All the way down the lane there is a tangle of campion and hedge-parsley on either side, until, passing three deserted cottages and an old life-boat house, one comes suddenly to the Cove, a little beach with fishing-boats drawn up, and a triangle of the bluest sea framed by a bluff of cliff to right and left.

Following an upward instinct one climbs the steeper cliff path on the left. The close-cropped grass is springy to the tread. In April it was covered with the vernal squill as with a blue mist, for the dainty little flowers, blue-grey on a ruddy stem, were starred in profusion everywhere. Now only the transparent seeds are left, standing two inches high, like tiny silver ghosts.

There on the top of the cliff, with sky and water for one's world, the thoughts aroused in that little grey church return ; thoughts of mortality and longings after immortality. And then the breaking waves of that infinite sea, relentless yet somehow reassuring, bring a message of death in life and life in death. The wave ends, but the sea remains and will remain.

C. C. ROGERS.
Church Cove

THESE things are for our son to know :
   The Lizard Light, a circling sword,
Trebarwith tide in crumbled snow,
   A wayward brook, a valley ford,
      Restormel, when June stands upon the keep,
      High seneschal of summer ; larches' sway
    In spinneys of Pencarrow, and the sweep
    And flash of wings above Port Isaac Bay.

   Truly these things are his. Then let him know
    Tranquil St. Tudy, Landewednack trees,
Furze golden on Goonhilly. Let him grow
    On Cornish earth between the Cornish seas :
For all are his, the cliff, the moor,
   From dark Penwith to windy Rame,
The pebbled beach, the sandy shore—
   The accents of his Cornish name—
The field, the river, and the strand,
The freedom of his Cornish land.

J. C. TREWIN.
Cornish Boy

We say farewell, the half we never know
Of those who wave their hands, farewell ! farewell !
And so we fade to distance—it is well—
If we knew all we leave we could not go.
How many a heart beneath the wings of snow,
In quest of other lands wherein to dwell,
Has passed this headland conscious of a spell,
Yet never sighed and felt the full tear flow !
These have not known that here the swallow first
Bears England summer on her glossy wings,
How first about this cape the cuckoo calls,
How here upon these southern-hearted walls
The earliest flowers to radiant glory burst,
And all day long of home the skylark sings.

H. D. RAWNSLEY.
Farewell at Lizard Point

If all the seas that ever sucked the hue
From midmost heaven, about dark rocks were rolled,
If all the winds that ever gathered gold
From out sea-air, upon their foreheads blew,
If all the wings of ocean birds that flew,
Milk-white upon the ledges dropped to fold—
Then, Kynance, would thy wave-bound fortress hold
Blue-girt, gold-washed, wing-whitened, rise to view.
Dear to the sailor passing up the Sound,
Dear to the wanderers as they westward rove,
Landewednack's cape, Landewednack's double eye ;
But, from Carthethra to St. Levan's bound,
No rocks so magical as those that lie
The Tawny lion-guards of Kynance Cove.

H. D. RAWNSLEY.
The Gull Rock
Kynance Cove

" RADIANT autumn it is indeed this year. Never was there such a September. All the hillsides are blazing with a glory of red and gold.

Purple of the rustling heather, gold of the scented gorse, mauve of the starry-flowered ling, russet of dying bracken. Mingled with all that brilliancy are clumps of the dead brown heather-bells that rustle as you touch them, rustle with a sound reminiscent of wind and sunshine and fragrance, the music of the wild country.

Here and there the late blooming heather mingles with the gorse in familiar undergrowth at your feet, forming a rich, mosaic pattern with detailed points of light. These catch the eye, but only those broad masses of distant colour can satisfy the soul with a blinding rush of ecstasy ; now and then in some hollow between the hills is a vivid pool of gold, where a gorse covert is in full bloom ; now and then a stretch of straw yellow, where the half-starved moorland grass has already taken on its winter garb ; and everywhere, to north and south and west, the blue sea. Sometimes a grey rock, sometimes the golden furze, plumb against the blue.

The colour of the sea is never out of your sight, the sound of it never out of your ears. The very air has a fresh, sea-blown taste. And in your being reigns a sense of power and freedom and joy ; joy that will never be exhausted, joy that you never can express."

C. C. ROGERS.

From The Giant's Carn

THE shore-lights curve in a warm, friendly arc,
Reflected in the black heave of an oil-smooth sea ;
Lamped shapes of moving sister-ships loom eerily.
The tilted, orange half-moon flares on headlands dark.

Under our rocking mast-light, by its mellow glow,
Five cloth-capped men in oilskins pull at the brown net ;
Dropping the silvery-burnished pilchards shining wet
In gathering heaps on deck, with customary rhythm slow.

E

They throw few rigid mackerel carelessly aside,
Irised in saxe, green, bellies sunset red ;
Strangled in cruel mesh those gleaming fishes dead,
Some still alive, bright fruit drawn from the sombre tide.

A following fleet of noisy, greedy birds,
Gulls in arrested, fluttering, dove-like, stooping flight,
Feet hanging, brilliant white, dark sudden in the night,
Swoop at the net ; with clamour drown men's shouted words.

Seven silver Pleiads climb above the paling moon,
Herself upon the wave, casting a shivered, silver bar,
Tide's limitary lover ! A liquid, sliding star.
No mystery full as Night's ; nor music deep as the Sea's tune.

JOSEPH BRADDOCK.

Fishing at Night
(*Mount's Bay*)

    ROBIN Hood and Little John
      They both are gone to the fair, O !
  And we will go to the merry greenwood
      To see what they do there, O :
        And for the chase, O—
  To chase for the buck and doe,
        With hale an tow, rum below ;*
        For we were up as soon as day, O,
        And for to fetch the summer home,
        The summer and the may, O ;
        For summer is a come, O,
        And winter is a gone, O.

* "Hale an tow" is a very ancient traditional burden.

Where are those Spaniards
  That make so great a boast, O ?
They shall eat the grey goose feather,
  And we will eat the roast, O,
    In every land, O,
The land where'er we go.
  As for George, O,
    Saint George he was a knight, O,
Of all the knights in Christendom,
  Saint George is the right, O.
    In every land, O,
    The land where'er we go.

God bless Aunt Mary Moses,**
  With all his power and might, O ;
And send us peace in merry England
  Both day and night, O !
And send us peace in merry England
  Both now and evermore, O !

TRADITIONAL.

Helston Furry Day Song

WHAT thing is harder than the rock ?
What softer is than water cleare ?
Yet wyll the same, with often droppe,
The hard rock perce as doth a spere.
Even so, nothing so hard to attayne,
But may be hadde, with labour and payne.

TRADITIONAL

Perseverance

(One of a series of ancient inscriptions
on panels in Pengersick Castle, near
Helston, Cornwall.)

** "Aunt Mary " is a Cornish and quite reverent term for the Virgin.

St. Michael's Mount, the tidal isle,
  In May with daffodils and lilies
Is kirtled gorgeously a while
    As ne'er another English hill is :
  About the precipices cling
  The rich renascence robes of Spring.

Her gold and silver, nature's gifts,
  The prodigal with both hands showers :
O not in patches, not in drifts
    But round and round, a mount of flowers—
  Of lilies and daffodils,
  The envy of all other hills.

And on the lofty summit looms
  The castle : none could build or plan it.
The foursquare foliage springs and blooms,
    The piled elaborate flowers of granite,
  That not the sun can wither ; no,
  Nor any tempest overthrow.

JOHN DAVIDSON.
St. Michael's Mount

Majestic Michael rises—he whose brow
Is crowned with castles, and whose rocky sides
Are clad with dusky ivy ; he whose base,
Beat by the storms of ages, stands unmoved
Amidst the wreck of things—the change of time.
That base, encircled by the azure waves
Was once with verdure clad ; the towering oaks
Here waved their branches green—the sacred oaks,
Whose awful shades among the Druids strayed
To cut the hallowed mistletoe, and hold
High converse with their gods.

SIR HUMPHRY DAVY, 1779—1829.
St. Michael's Mount

" Ay me ! whilst thee the shores and sounding seas
Wash far away,—where'er thy bones are hurl'd,
Whether beyond the stormy Hebrides
Where thou perhaps, under the whelming tide,
Visitest the bottom of the monstrous world ;
Or whether thou, to our moist vows denied,
Sleep'st by the fable of Bellerus old,
Where the great Vision of the guarded mount
Looks towards Namancos and Bayona's hold,
—Look homeward, Angel, now, and melt with ruth :
—And, O ye dolphins, waft the hapless youth !"

JOHN MILTON.
From *Lycidas*

GREY watcher of the changeful tides that press
Above the buried shores of Lyonesse—
Lone sentinel that stands
Girdled with sands—
Around thy vigils dreamily
Washes the Cornish sea,
And laughing Springtime all about thee spills
Her early primroses and daffodils.

Sometimes aloof from a phantasmal coast
Thou gloomest in the fog, a sheeted ghost ;
Sometimes the morning's rose
Quivers and glows,
Or westering sunlight's vision of desire
Sets thee afire,
While lazily the boats around thy quay
Sway to the seabirds and the lapping sea.

But when the clouds with sullen doomful black
Have piled their massy bulwarks at thy back,
And the swift sundown lights
Thy pinnacled heights.
Thou art an altar scrolled
With letters of gold—
Flash of the Eternal on a secular doom,
Love soaring stainless from a sea of gloom.

A. L. SALMON
St. Michael's Mount

ON the sea
The sunbeams tremble, and the purple light
Illumes the dark Bolerium, seat of storms.
High are his granite rocks, his frowning brow
Hangs o'er the smiling ocean. In his caves
The Atlantic breezes murmur ; in his caves,
Where sleep the haggard spirits of the storm.
Wild, dreary, are the frowning rocks around,
Encircled by the wave, where to the breeze
The haggard cormorant shrieks ; and far beyond,
Where the great ocean mingles with the sky,
Are seen the cloud-like islands, grey in mist.

SIR HUMPHRY DAVEY.
On Land's End

The following verses were inspired by the finding of an Indian cowrie in a barrow at Land's End.

" WHAT year was it that blew
The Aryan's wicker-work canoe
Which brought the shell to English land ?
What prehistoric man or woman's hand,
With what intent, consigned it to this grave—
This barrow set in sound of the Ancient World's last wave ?

Beside it in the mound
A charmèd bead of flint was found.
Some woman surely in this place
Covered with flowers a little baby-face,
And laid the cowrie on the cold dead breast ;
And, weeping, turned for comfort to the landless West.

*   *   *

No man shall ever know
It happened all so long ago
That this same childless woman may
Have stood upon the cliffs around the bay
And watched for tin-ships that no longer came,
Nor knew that Carthage had gone down in Roman flame."

W. CANTON.

BESIDE the clock two spaniels stand,
Two china spaniels, golden spotted.
On a lace doily (contraband)
Beams a red-faced geranium (potted).

Framed portraits rest on woollen mats,
Black-bearded smugglers with their spouses,
The gentlemen wear bowler hats,
The ladies sport their Sunday blouses,

Two pictures decorate the wall,
Vesuvius, spouting sparks and ashes,
The brig " Calypso " in a squall,
Full-sailed despite the lightning flashes.

Without, the dark Atlantic flings
Against the cliff its booming surges,
And, as a shell, this snug room rings
With its reverberating dirges.

Shaking the door the night winds whine,
Like outcast mongrels shrill and shifting.
Seaward, the tossing ship-lights shine,
Ruby and green, like fire-flies drifting.

CROSBIE GARSTIN.
A Cornish Cottage

On Newlyn Hill the gorse is bright ;
    Upon the hedge-rows left and right
Song-dizzy birds the spring-time greet ;
The bluebells weave a purple sheet ;
    Primroses star the lane's green night.

Across the Bay each moorland height
Glows golden in the evening light,
And dusk walks violet-eyed and sweet
    On Newlyn Hill.

A swarm of lights, pearl-soft and white,
A fairy-lamp-land exquisite,
Opens its star-eyes at the feet
Of hills where sky and wavelets meet.
Then dreams come, mystic, infinite,
    On Newlyn Hill.

CROSBIE GARSTIN.
Rondeau

FLASHED Lizard to Bishop
" They're rounding the fish up
Close under my cliffs where the cormorants nest,
   The lugger lamps glitter
   In hundreds and litter
The sea-floor like spangles. What news from the West?"

Flashed he of the mitre
" The night's growing brighter,
There's mist over Annet, but all's clear at sea.
   Lit up like a city,
   Her band playing pretty,
A big liner's passing. Aye, all's well with me."

Flashed Wolf to Round Island,
" Oh you upon dry land,
With wild rabbits cropping the pinks at your base,
   You lubber, you oughter
   Stand watch in salt water,
With tides tearing at you and spray in your face."

The gun of the Longships
Boomed out like a gong—" Ships
Are bleating around me like sheep gone astray.
   There's fog in my channel
   As thick as grey flannel—
Boom—rumble!—I'm busy. Excuse me, I pray."

They winked at each other,
   As brother to brother,
Those red lights and white lights, the summer night through.
   And steered the stray tramps out,
   Till dawn snuffed their lamps out,
And stained the sea meadows all purple and blue.

CROSBIE GARSTIN.
The Sea-lights
(*Isles of Scilly*)

" OLD woman, old woman, old woman," said I,
" 'Tis a mighty queer place to be building a home,
In the teeth of the gales and the wash of the foam,
With nothing in view but the sea and the sky ;
It cannot be cheerful, or healthy, or dry.
Why don't you go inland and rent a snug house
With fowls in the garden and blossoming boughs,
Old woman, old woman, old woman ?" said I.

" A garden have I at my hand
    Beneath the green swell,
With pathways of glimmering sand
    And borders of shell.
There twinkle the star-fish and there
    Red jellies unfold.
The weed banners ripple and flare,
    All purple and gold,
And have I no poultry ? Oh come
    When the Equinox lulls,
The air is a-flash and a-hum
    With the tumult of gulls,
They whirl in a shimmering cloud
    Sun-bright on the breeze,
They perch on my chimneys and crowd
    To nest at my knees,
And set their dun chickens to rock on the motherly
    Lap of the seas."

" Old woman, old woman, old woman," said I,
" It sounds very well but it cannot be right,
This must be a desolate spot of a night,
With nothing to hear but the guillemot's cry,
The sob of the surf and the wind soughing by.
Go inland and get you a cat for your knee,
And gather your gossips for scandal and tea,
Old woman, old woman, old woman," said I.

" No amber-eyed tabby may laze
    And purr at my feet,
But here in the blue summer days
    The seal people meet.
They bask on my ledges and romp
    In the swirl of the tides,
Old bulls with their whiskers and pomp
    And sleek little brides.
Yet others come visiting me
    Than grey seal or bird,
Men come in the night from the sea
    And utter no word,
Wet weed clings to bosom and hair,
    Their faces are drawn,
They crouch by my embers and stare,
    And go with the dawn
To sleep in my garden, the swell flowing over them
    Like a green lawn."

CROSBIE GARSTIN.
Old Woman's House Rock
(*Isles of Scilly*)

IN sea-cold Lyonesse,
When the Sabbath eve shafts down
On the roofs, walls, belfries
Of the foundered town,
The Nereids pluck their lyres
Where the green translucency beats,
And with motionless eyes at gaze
Make minstrelsy in the streets.
And the ocean water stirs
In salt-worn casement and porch.
Plies the blunt-snouted fish
With fire in his skull for torch.

And the ringing wires resound ;
And the unearthly lovely weep,
In lament of the music they make
In the sullen courts of sleep :
Whose marble flowers bloom for aye :
And—tapped by the moon-guiled tide—
Mock their carver with heart of stone,
Caged in his stone-ribbed side.

WALTER DE LA MARE.
Sunk Lyonesse

SHE bade me to a garden far to south
In blue-sea'd Lyonesse, that fabled shore,
Where nectarine and peach warm to the mouth
And soft-bloomed plum the ripening branches bore.

But walking through the harvest golden-sheaved
Toward the goal, the summer air lost will ;
No tremor stirred the great trees myriad-leaved,
It was a land where time and thought stood still.

Merlin had waved a wand ; the lake gleamed white ;
The house stood dark ; none moved about the ways ;
The garden, four-square walled, shone apple-bright
In a shut sleep death's pinions could not graze.

In every wall a door, and each door fast :
An Eden whence all mortal love was cast.

C. C. ABBOTT.
The Garden

" THERE are few tracks in England more rugged than the northern part of the peninsula that lies between the Land's End and St. Ives. It is possible to travel across the moors from Crobben Hill to Chapel Cairn Brea without setting foot on cultivated ground. It is a boulder-strewn waste, void of trees, where the grey of the granite mingles in spring and autumn with the gold of the gorse that, with heather and bracken, clothes the undulating surface . . .

To the lover of nature the wild aspect of these breezy uplands is not without its charm ; but the glory of the promontory is the ocean in which it is set. The great rampart of cliffs that holds back the Atlantic is broken here and there by beaches of white sand or minute shells, or by coves into which fall the trout-streams that rise in the granite hills above. Along the tangled valleys they water many an interesting picture arrests the eye ; but whether it be a holy well, an old mill, a grove, a rustic bridge or fishing-hamlet, all is in tender miniature, like the streams themselves or the modest hills where they bubble to the light."

J. C. TREGARTHEN.
West Cornwall

WITH a cold north wind and a cockled sea,
  Or an Autumn's cloudless day,
At the Huer's bid to stem we row,
  Or upon our paddles play.
All the signs, East, West, and Quiet,
  *Could Roos, too well know we !

Chorus :

  We can bend a stop, secure a cross,
    For brave sean lads are we.
  We can bend a stop, secure a cross,
    For brave sean lads are we.

* " Cast net."

If we have first stem when " he-va " comes,
 We'll the Huer's bushes watch ;
We will row right off or quiet lie,
 Flying summer sculls to catch.
And when he winds the tow boat round,
 We will all ready be ;

Chorus :

  When he gives " Could Roos " we'll shout " Hurrah "
   For merry sean lads are we !
  When he gives " Could Roos " we'll shout " Hurrah "
   For merry sean lads are we !

When the sean we've shot, upon the tow
 We will heave with all our might,
With a " Heave ! Heave O !" and " Rouse ! Rouse O !"
 Till the huer cries "All right."
Then on the bunt place kegs and weights,
 And next to tuck we go !

Chorus :

  We'll dip, and trip, with a " Hip Hurrah !"
   For merry sean lads are we !
  We'll dip, and trip, with a " Hip Hurrah !"
   For merry sean lads are we !

C. TAYLOR STEVENS
Seaners' (or *Seiners'*) *Song*

" THE Sayne is a net, of about fortie fathoms in length, with which they encompasse a part of the Sea, and drawe the same on land by two ropes, fastned at his ends, together with such fish as lighteth within his precinct . . .

The Sayne, is in fashion, like that within harbour, but of a farre larger proportion. To each of these, there commonly belong three or foure boates, carrying about six men apeece : with which, when the season of the yeere and weather serveth, they lie hovering upon the coast, and are directed in their worke, by a Balker, or Huer, who standeth on the Cliffe side, and from thence, best discerneth the quantitie and course of the Pilchard : according whereunto, hee cundreth (as they call it) the Master of each boate (who hath his eye still fixed upon him) by crying with a lowd voice, whistling through his fingers, and wheazing certing diversified and significant signes, with a bush, which he holdeth in his hand. At his appointment they cast out there Net, draw it to either hand, as the Schoell lyeth, or fareth, beat with there Oares to keepe in the Fish, and at last, either close it and tucke it up in the Sea, or draw the same on land, with more certain profit, if the ground be not rough of rockes. After one companie have thus shot their Net, another beginneth behind them, and so a third, as oportunitie serveth. Being so taken, some, the Countrie people, who attend with their horses and paniers at the Cliffs side, in great numbers, do buy and carrie home, the larger remainder, is by the Marchant, greedily and speedily seized upon."

RICHARD CAREW, 1602.
The Sayne
From *The Survey of Cornwall*

THE corn is in the shock,
And the fish are on the rock,
And the merry boats go dancing out of Whitesand Bay,
    I hear the huer's cry,
      And I see the dappled sky,
And it minds me of the days that are long gone away.

The corn was in the shock
And the fish were on the rock,
And the sea was all alive from the Wolf to Castle Treen,
    But the fog came down by night,
    And it hid the Longships Light,
And the men that went afishing never, never more were seen.

The corn was in the shock,
And the fish were on the rock,
When the boats went out from Sennen with the pilchard seine ;
    But the morning broke so fair,
    And not a boat was there,
And the lad I lov'd was with them and he came not back again.

The corn is in the shock,
And the fish are on the rock,
And the golden sun is gleaming on the Islands of the West ;
    I hear the huer's cry,
    And I see the dappled sky,
But my heart is dead with sorrow for the lad I love the best.

KATHARINE LEE JENNER.
The Boats of Sennen
Cornish Fisher-girl's Song

THE half-forgotten music of old names
    Clings to the rocks and hills,
And an intangible human fragrance gives
    To senseless earth, and fills
With glamour half divine all the wild places,
    Recalling the old days,
When men on earth believed that the Divine
    Encompassed all his ways.

Out of the vast void of oblivion
    Rings the wild melody
Of those old words, whose only resting-place
    Is the vague memory
Of man, the creature so prone to forget,
    Yet who forgetting clings,
Subconsciously remembering their sense,
    To the old names and things.

The music of the old names is worn thin
    By busy lips of men ;
Yet they are eloquent of ancient dreams
    Of knightly valour, when
The hills were purpled and the valleys stained
    With battles and sore strife,
And of the deeds, achievements, hopes, and fears,
    Of long-forgotten life.

Come to Carn Brea, beside Trevorian Down,
    And hear the Gwynver call*
From Vellandreath, Carn Bargas, and Carn Ky,
    While evening shadows fall
On Tregonebris and Boscawen-Oon,
    And over Crows-an-Wra,
And on Bartinny and Caer Brane there shines
    The light of dying day.

Away beyond Rospannel and Boscarn
    And Buryan tower above,
The southern sea is gleaming through the gap
    That marks Lamorna Cove,
And all about St. Levan and Penberth
    On to Pedn-Men-an-Mere
The sunset shines upon a land whose names
    Are music everywhere.

* The " calling of the Gwynver " is the sound of the sea breaking upon Gwynver
Sands by Sennen. The story is that it is the sea moaning for the loss of Guinevere,
who escaped from it when Lyonnesse was submerged. Sometimes it can be
heard as far off as Penzance, and it betokens evil fortune.

These names of our dead speech are music still
  In our dear living land,
Which never can be void or desolate
  While here on every hand
Is still the record of our fathers' lives,
  Though their old hopes and fears
Have passed away like sunlight on the hills
  Down through the path of years.

KATHARINE LEE JENNER
(MRS. HENRY JENNER)
The Old Names

" PERHAPS I have said enough for you to understand why
this little tongue of land, whose tip is the Land's End, has got
such a hold upon me. On the greyest days the moors are not
dismal to me, nor the shores melancholy. There's hardly a
square mile out of the hundred that isn't full of associations.
The cliffs, the wastes of furze and heather, the tangled bottoms,
the open beaches and the little coves, are all rich in pleasant
memories ; and the whistle of the curlew, the croak of raven
or hern, the scream of the sea-fowl, the piping of small wading
birds and the song of the sedge-warbler, are to me the music
of familiar voices. Rolling veldt, mountain range and rivers
don't appeal to me like the downs, hills and streams that I've
got to know by heart.

'A treeless, barren waste' a man once called the Land's
End district to my poor father, who preferred the scent of the
furze to the perfume of roses and the bell-heather before
hot-house flowers. Everything wild he liked, ay, loved ; the
sea-pinks, the golden samphire, the sea-holly, the ferns, the
zawns, the seaweed in the pools, the shells on the beach. And
when he was unable to move out of the house—he lived to
eighty-two—he used to sit up in the little bay-window, where
he could see the sun set, and watch for my return, and then
he'd ask what birds I'd seen, and about the flowers. The
speedwell, the scarlet pimpernel, and the forgetmenot, were

special favourites of his, and I'd always bring home one or
the other in my fishing-basket. Touching it was to see him
look at them. If ever a man loved nature with his whole soul,
my father did, but above everything he loved the birds "

J. C. TREGARTHEN.

THIS is the sea. In these uneven walls
    A wave lies prisoned. Far and far away
Outward to ocean, as the slow tide falls
    Her sisters through the capes that hold the bay
Dancing in lovely liberty recede.
    Yet lovely in captivity she lies,
Filled with soft colours, where the waving weed
    Moves gently and discloses to our eyes
Blurred shining veins of rock and lucent shells
    Under the light-shot water ; and here repose
Small quiet fish and dimly glowing bells
    Of sleeping sea-anemones that close
Their tender fronds and will not now awake
Till on these rocks the waves returning break.

EDWARD SHANKS.
The Rock Pool

IN this water, clear as air,
Lurks a lobster in its lair.
Rock-bound weed sways out and in,
Coral-red, and bottle-green.
Wondrous pale anemones
Stir like flowers in a breeze :
Fluted scallop, whelk in shell,
And the prowling mackerel.
Winged with snow the sea-mews ride
The brine-keen wind ; and far and wide
Sounds on the hollow thunder of the tide.

WALTER DE LA MARE.
The Pool in the Rock

THE green cliffs are sweet with gorse ; the scent,
The sunbright spendthrift beauty of it, spilling down
To the sea's edge ; and all ways the green
Is sewn with bluebells and windflowers and celandine,
Like tapestry. O heart, heart, this is content !
This is the final crown
Of happiness ; this is to stand on the pinnacle of peace.

The sea below is fathomless, as full of light
As ever in memory ; that piercing blue
Still far outmatches the matchless robe of heaven,
And the curve of the coast is the same as the eye has seen
In dreams, sleeping and waking.
The cries of the gulls are blown on the wind for ever ; they
          never cease ;
And the high headland, where the surf is breaking,
Lies in the sun unchanged, unchanging, yet new,
And balm to the eyes that have longed for its sweet sight.

They fall away like clouds, the years that are past . . .
O heart, know your haven,
And one who walks as a man walks in his own green land at
          last.

                                        M. E. RHODES
                                        Pinnacle

" TOUCHING the temperature of *Cornwall,* the ayre thereof is cleansed, as with bellowes, by the billowes, and flowing and ebbing of the Sea, and therethrough becometh pure, and subtill, and, by consequence, healthfull . . .

The Spring visiteth not these quarters so timely, as the Easterne parts. Summer imparteth a verie temperate heat, recompencing his slow fostering of the fruit, with their kindly ripening. Autumn bringeth a somewhat late Harvest, specially to the middle of the Shire, where they seldom cut their corn before Michaelmas. Winter, by reason of the Southes neere neighbourhead, and seas warme breath, favoureth it with a milder cold than elsewhere, so as, upon both coastes, the Frost and Snow come verie seldome, and make a speedie departure. This notwithstanding, the Countrie is much subject to stormes, which fetching a large course in the open Sea, doe from thence violently assault the dwellers at land, and leave them uncovered houses, pared hedges, and dwarfe-growne trees, as witness of their force and furie : yea, even the hard stones, and yron barres of the windowes, doe fret to be so continually grated. One kind of these storms, they call a flaw or flaugh, which is a mighty gale of wind, passing suddainely to the shore, and working strong effects, upon whatsoever it incountreth in his way."

RICHARD CAREW, 1602.
From "*The Survey of Cornwall*"

Catch in a crucible a crystal drop
Flying from waves in foam-enchanted spray.
Watch wavelets creep into the inward pools,
Leaving the wilder sea for gentler play.
Gaze into pools and watch the seaweed flow,
Dark like the twining tendrils of thick hair,
Or juicy green, or pink and filigree.
Gaze deeper, through the limpid water, where
The shells and pebbles show a brighter hue
Because the mirrored depths hold colour trapped.
Then, from close peering, raise the head and gaze
At distant cliffs, where heather banks are wrapped
About with green and brown, above the brown
And black and gold of lichen-crusted rocks.
Watch now the glint of sun on wings—small birds
From landwards seaward wend in flocks ;
And gulls swoop singly now, and now in pairs ;
Or in a concourse crowd about one place
And scream and whirl and fight—then seaward trace
Their curved and easy flight on eddied winds.
Now back to breakers thundering on the shore,
Watching the crystal greens and deeper blues.
The eyes are held. And all the soul once more
Surges in joy and revels in escape,
Borne on the wave in wildness to its end,
Dancing in white and drowning in the green,
Losing itself where all sea-colours blend.
Each drop—each gull—each shade in the rich deep,
Each wealthy moment on the shore will be
Absorbed into the essence of your life,
Until in very truth, you are the sea.

LORNA L. HAWKEY.
Cornwall

FIRST there were two of us, then there were three of us,
Then there was one bird more,
Four of us—wild white sea-birds,
Treading the ocean floor ;
And the *wind* rose, and the *sea* rose,
To the angry billows' roar—
With one of us—two of us—three of us, four of us
Sea-birds on the shore.

Soon there were five of us, soon there were nine of us,
And lo ! in a trice sixteen !
And the yeasty surf curdled over the sands,
The gaunt grey rocks between ;
And the tempest raved, and the lightning's fire
Struck blue on the spindrift hoar—
And on four of us—ay, and on four times four of us
Sea-birds on the shore.

And our sixteen waxed to thirty-two,
And they to past three-score—
A wild, white welter of winnowing wings,
And ever more and more ;
And the winds lulled, and the sea went down,
And the sun streamed out on high,
Gilding the pools and the spume and the spars
'Neath the vast blue deeps of the sky ;

And the isles and the bright green headlands shone,
As they'd never shone before,
Mountains and valleys of silver cloud,
Wherein to swing, sweep, soar—
A host of screeching, scolding, scrabbling
Sea-birds on the shore—
A snowy, silent, sun-washed drift
Of sea-birds on the shore.

WALTER DE LA MARE.
The Storm

A dusk-dimmed silence wrapped my sitting-room
Except at the focal point where blazed
And crackled a salt-saturated spar
Of storm wood ; gurgling upwards from sea deeps,
Lending an hour of delight before dwindling
To a handful of ash ; this old oak knee
That was hewn in its light-leaf beauty and strength
Perhaps two hundred years ago, and maybe too
It flourished in the forest a century before
It felt the blade of the woodman's axe ;
And since that day of tragedy has tossed
On the waves where it braced the beams of a leaping ship ;
Then under water as a brine-soaked wreck
Upon the turbulent ocean floor. Now my hearth
Is flickered with a thousand jewelled flames,
Fire opal jets and blue-green peacock spears,
In-gathered from the phosphorescent sea ;
And as I gazed my fancy idly wended
To times before lighthouses stood to guard
Our granite coasts : nights when the wrought-iron cressets
Flared on the flocculent foam, hand-fed
By men who salvaged this old ship-timber
Shored by spring tides, and heaped in readiness
For kindling with faggots of furze and bracken,
To light the wandering mariner safe home
Past Land's End, Lizard, magnetic Manacles . . .
Those days are over and so with mind at ease
I could enjoy upon that stormy evening
Within my sheltered room, the glowing oak
That once again it seemed became a tree,
Sprouting green flames as living leaves in Spring,
And flaming leaves for Autumn's farewell gold.

GLADYS HUNKIN.
Storm Spar

THE following set of verses is a collection of the names of places in Cornwall, arranged in alternate rhyme by Mr. Davies Gilbert (1767-1839) born at St. Erth, to show the euphony of the ancient Cornish tongue.

Velandrukya Cracka Cudna,
Truzemenhall Chun Crowzanwrah,
Bans Burnnhal Brane Bosfrancan,
Treeve Trewhidden Try Trembah.

Carn Kanidgrac Castle-Skudjiac,
Beagle Tuben Amalvear,
Amalebria Amalwhidden,
Skillewadden Trink Polpeor.

Pellalith Pellallawortha,
Buzzavean Chyponds Boswase,
Ventongrimps Roskestal Raftra,
Hendra Grancan Treen Bostraze.

Treganebris Embla Bridgia,
Menadarver Treveneage,
Tregaminion Fouge Trevidgia,
Gwarnick Trewy Reskajeage.

Luggans Vellanvoane Treglisson,
Gear Noongumpus Helan gove,
Carnequidden Brea Bojoncan,
Dryn Chykembra Dowran Trove.

Menagwithers Castlegotha,
Carnongrease Trevespanvean,
Prazeanbeeble Main Trebarva,
Bone Trengwainton Lethargwean.

Stablehobba Balaswhidden,
Tringey Trannack Try Trenear,
Fraddam Crowlas Gwallan Crankan,
Drift Bojedna Cayle Trebear.

Haltergantic Carnaliezy,
Gumford Brunion Nancekeage,
Reen Trevesken Mevagizzy,
Killow Carbus Carn Tretheage.

DAVIES GILBERT
Cornish Nonsense Verse

WHEN Sam goes back in memory,
    It is to where the sea
Breaks on the shingle, emerald-green
    In white foam, endlessly :
He says—with small brown eye on mine—
    " I used to keep awake,
And lean from my window in the moon,
    Watching those billows break.
And half a million tiny hands,
    And eyes, like sparks of frost,
Would dance and come tumbling into the moon,
    On every breaker tossed.
And all across from star to star,
    I've seen the watery sea,
With not a single ship in sight,
    Just ocean there, and me ;
And heard my father snore . . . And once,
    As sure as I'm alive,
Out of those wallowing, moon-flecked waves
    I saw a mermaid dive ;

Head and shoulders above the wave,
    Plain as I now see you,
Combing her hair, now back, now front,
    Her two eyes peeping through ;
Calling me, ' Sam !'—quietlike—' Sam !' . . .
    But me . . . I never went,
Making believe I kind of thought
    'Twas someone else she meant . . .
Wonderfully lovely there she sat,
    Singing the night away,
All in the solitudinous sea
    Of that there lonely bay.
" P'raps," and he'd smooth his hairless mouth,
" P'raps, if 'twere *now*, my son,
P'raps, if I heard a voice say, ' Sam !' . . .
    Morning would find me gone."

WALTER DE LA MARE.
Sam

I

To the gold, to the gold
Of the sunset we fly !
All silver the streams
    That glide through the green :
Black are the trees
That with tracery dark
Lean from the hill-top
Athwart the clear sky ;
White plumes that float by
Mark our swift flight,
To the gold of the sunset,
And on to the night.

*By Train to the West
(Winter)*

II

SUNLIGHT on the little shore,
Turns grey to silver, and the white
Of foam to dazzling snow.
The distance sombre is no more
But springs with colour into light ;
And from the rocks below,
Touched as they fly, with rainbow hue,
Sea-flowers of spume drift floating by ;
Each little pool, an eye of blue,
Gives back its colour to the sky.
Gone leaden grey of winter cold,
Washed all the air with liquid gold.

Winter Sunshine in Cornwall

III

I know a valley fair that gently winds
To folded hills above the western sea ;
Brown now the new-ploughed earth that crowns those hills ;
For Spring has laid her warm caressing hand
Upon the earth ; and all the valley slopes
Are dusted with the faint, sweet, yellow dust
Of primroses among their tender green.
Bright celandines in constellations shine,
Like golden stars in polished splendour gleaming,
Of cloth of gold in sunlight richly spread.
High on the bank a clump of blackthorn grows,
And now each twig, frosted with starry flowers,
Makes snow where none has lain the winter through ;
For mild that valley lies towards the sea,
Now blue and clear, and edged with spreading lace
Of twinkling wavelets breaking into foam.
At every season is that valley fair,
But loveliest now, or when at harvest-time

The hills are crowned with gold of waving corn,
And as the sunset-rays rest lovingly
Upon the valley's slopes, they turn to rose,
And glow as if all summer's warmth were gathered there.

Cornish Valley in Spring

IV

WHAT flower on earth so tells of Spring as does the primrose
    pale ?
Earth's green, the green of Spring, tender and new,
Is in her leaves ; her petals, heaven's light
Softened with green ; for luminous they glow,
And in their heart burns the warm golden sun,
While round them, soft and cool, the crinkled leaves
All diamonded with dew of morning, lie
In freshness delicate.

Primroses

V

Upon the cliff's warm slope where sea-pinks grow,
I lie and sideways lean my head, when lo !
Like window opening into Paradise,
The scene is nearer drawn, and stretched below,
In silken sheen that swims before my gaze,
The sea lies gleaming in translucent haze.

No purple shadows o'er its surface stray,
No lace of spreading foam, no flying spray,
With rainbow flashes upon it now ;
No changing lights of Spring upon it play,
But mist and light are merged until the blue
Is summer's warmest and most tender hue.

June Morning on the Cornish Cliffs
MARGARET BONE.
Cornish Year

ABOVE the green and curving brow
Of the bright valley's sunlit steep,
Like some old warrior, grey and lone,
On solitary mound, a stone
Looks out unchanged across the deep.

Through centuries of change, yet still
From dark green blades of bluebell leaves,
Down the long slope, primroses show
Their yellow-green, while far below
In long, slow swells the Atlantic heaves.

Through centuries of change—of war,
Havoc, and death, and human pain,
He stands. Sometimes into his sky
Come giant man-made birds that fly,
And swoop, and dive, and mount again.

That haunt of peace, that valley fair
Shows but the change the seasons bring,
The flowery cycle of the year ;
From the pale primrose, to the mist
Of blue and rose and amethyst
The bluebell and the campion fling
Along the slopes ; till foxgloves lean
Stately and tall, each one a queen,
Soon to be lost amid the deeps
Of bracken-forests darkly green.

Heedless of all, his watch he keeps
That lone grey form, the ages through ;
Afar he looks, where grey or blue,
Moves, lifting, swaying endlessly,
The unchanged, ever-changing sea.

MARGARET BONE.
The Lonely Warrior

WHEN parched July has powdered down
Flaked dust upon the tired town,
A small smooth-bouldered rockery
Lures from the shade to comfort me
With touch of water-moulded stone,
And tufted sea-thrift all full-blown.
I need but close my eyes to know
That on its home cliffs breezes blow,
Just as they did one summer day
Where tapered Five Points stretch away,
Dabbling long fingers in white spray,
From Clodgy Point to far Trevail.
To see close-clinging to the shale
On toughened root, the lance-like leaves
In round and tightly crowded sheaves,
Thrusting on upright stem each bloom,
Together massed a smouldering plume
Of flame, shell-petalled, peach and rose
The undulating colour flows.
Its own faint scent comes drifting near
And papery rustle on my ear
Sifts through the sound of traffic thick,
And by the soul's arithmetic
I bridge the arid miles between
This garden and that precious scene,
And go to walk beneath cool skies
To fill my hands and feast my eyes.

GLADYS HUNKIN.
Sea Pinks in a City Garden

NINE merry maidens
Dancing all together,
Dancing all the Sabbath day
In the summer weather.
Larks in the blue sky,
Flowers in the grass,
Censing all the summer air
As they pass.
And an old man whispers low,
" See the maidens how they go,
Dancing hither, dancing thither,
Dancing, dancing any whither,
Flouting in their pagan glee
My respectability !
Maidens you should all beware,
Though the censers swing in air,
And the myriad sacring bell
Of the heather tinkles well,
Yet these cannot render you
Innocent in all you do ;
Maidens whither ends your dance
When night and winter shall advance ?

*   *   *

Nine grey stones,
On the moorland bare,
And grey wraiths wavering through
The corridors of air.
Through the cold corridors,
Whisht and lost,
They are feeling
Their way wind-tost.
Wind-tost and twisted sore,
Writhing shapes, now no more
The fragrant rose her censer swings,
No sacring bell the heather rings ;
Like churches when one lingers late
All the hills lie desolate.

Oh misty sprites, and bodies cold
Of greying stones, what have you told
The wailing winds, that still they cry
Your sorrows to the passer-by ?
" We who lived and danced in the sun
Into the dark went one by one
As you shall when your day is done."

ANNE TRENEER.
Nine Maidens : *Bosullow Common*

As the dull waves
    Of a sullen sea
Flash sapphire and silver
    Into glory,

And icy earth
    Grows soft to beget
The cyclamen
    And wild violet,

So after night
    Of hideous war,
Above the ruin
    Shines a star

Where, rudely sheltered
    From the wind and the rain,
The Son of Man
    Is born again.

ANNE TRENEER.
Christmas, 1946

G

Now in the waning of summer these stony moorlands
  Are purple and gold with gorse and mingled heath,
The brambles down by the beck are black with berries,
  Fostered by suns overhead and the waters beneath.

The path we tread is a sheep track buried in heather,
  Or an old Celt road with cart-ruts scoring the way,
Till the steep last rise is passed, and shining below us
  The harbour thrusts like a scimitar into the bay.

Happy it is to go back to a place remembered,
  To watch it change and unfold as the road winds down ;
Each name on lintel and wall is a voice to call us
  Through alley and tumbling lane to the heart of the town.

There's wind in the harbour and white-tipped waves, masts
      rocking,
  A high tide running atilt at the gray sea-wall,
A dancing boat with the sun in her sails bound seaward,
  And the white gulls flying and crying over all.

This simple country, stern, belovéd Cornwall,
  Purged by the winds, clean-mated with the sea,
This coloured corner of England—O earth-caged spirit,
  This is your heaven—spread wings, come forth, come free !

                                        P. H. B. LYON.
                                        A Country Holiday

          THE little meadow by the sand,
          Where Tamsin lies, is ringed about
          With acres of the scented thyme.
          The salt wind blows in all the land ;
          The great clouds pace across the skies ;
          Rare wanderers from the ferry climb.
          One might sleep well enough, no doubt,
            Where Tamsin lies.

Tamsin has sunshine now and wind,
And all in life she might not have,
The silence and the utter peace
That tempest-winnowed spirits find
On slopes that front the western wave.
The white gulls circle without cease
O'er Tamsin's grave.

E. K. CHAMBERS.
Lelant
(In Memory of Thomasine Trenoweth, aged 23.)

" Go down to Cornwall. There's a village there, perfect—
St. Mawgan in the Vale of Lanherne—so old, so quiet, all
hidden among the trees, with a Perpendicular tower older
than America.

Then go to Newquay and sit on Pentire Head, all gorse
and golden samphire, in summer, as I remember it—sea
extraordinarily wide and purple."

SINCLAIR LEWIS.
From *Ann Vickers*

" WHEN I come home to die I shall not feel that I have lived
in vain. I have seen the earth turn red at evening, the dew
sparkling in the morning, and the snow shining under a
frosty sun ; I have smelt the rain after drought, and have
heard the stormy Atlantic beat upon the granite shores of
Cornwall."

BERTRAND RUSSELL.
From *The Scientific Outlook*

AFTER the plow
The sea-gulls follow,
Up the hill
And down the hollow,

A cloud of wings,
A storm of cries,
That rise and fall,
That fall and rise,

Where the slow brown furrow
Rolls from the share
The sea-gulls hover,
Their pale eyes stare.

At the fluid earth
They stare and scream,
White breasts above
The slow brown stream,

And the plowman thinks
Of his youth again,
And a high dark wave
With a horse's mane.

ELIZABETH J. COATSWORTH.
St. Eval

SHARP blade of the prevailing Western wind
　　Chiselled the moorland thorn
Persistently until it disciplined
　　Soft twigs the parent stem had borne ;
Trimmed, slashed, and shaped until the full-grown tree
　　To fend such ruthless harsh attack,
Leaned over in its gnarled deformity
　　And turned an aged and curving back.
Incredible that anything so old
　　Could wake with buds on every limb,

Cascades of whitest blossom to unfold.
With secret tears my eyes grow dim
Recalling now past days of searing pain,
So cut and buffeted by life ;
O could my heart break through its grief again
And like this tree forget its strife.

GLADYS HUNKIN.
The Windswept Thorn

O d'you hear the seas complainin', and complainin', while it's
rainin' ?
Did you hear it mourn in the dimorts, when the surf woke up
and sighed ?
The choughs screamed on the sand,
And the foam flew over land,
And the seas flew dark on the Doom-Bar at rising of the tide.

I gave my lad a token, when he left me nigh heart-broken,
To mind him of old Padstow town, where loving souls abide ;
'Twas a ring with the words set
All round, " Can Love Forget ?"
And I watched his vessel toss on the Bar with the outward
turning tide.

D'you hear the seas complainin', and complainin', while it's
rainin' ?
And his vessel has never crossed the Bar from the puple seas
outside ;
And down the shell-pink sands,
Where we once went, holding hands,
Alone I watch the Doom-Bar and the rising of the tide.

One day—'twas four days after—the harbour-girls, with
    laughter,
So soft and wild as sea-gulls when they're playing seek-and-
    hide,
      Coaxed me out—for tide were lower
      Than had ever been known before ;
And we ran across the Doom-Bar, all white and shining wide.

I saw a something shinin', where the long wet weeds were
    twinin',
Around a rosy scallop ; and a gold ring lay inside ;
      And around its rim were set
      The words, " Can Love Forget ?"
And there upon the Doom-Bar I knelt and sobbed and cried.

I took my ring and smoothed it where the sands and shells
    had grooved it ;
But O ! St. Petroc bells will never ring me home a bride !—
      For the night my lad was leavin'
      Me, all tearful-eyed and grievin'
He had tossed my keepsake out on the Bar to the rise and fall
    of the tide !

D'you hear the seas complainin', and complainin', while it's
    rainin' ?
Did you hear them call in the dimorts when the surf woke up
    and sighed ?
      Maybe it is a token
      I shall get no more heart-broken—
And I shall cross the Doom-Bar at the turning of the tide.

ALICE E. GILLINGTON.
The Doom-bar

STRANGE that this shy and gentle bird should choose
To build its nest within the tidal caves
Of granite coasts, where mighty ocean spues
In spindrift, tossed from crests of mounting waves.
Storm-buffeted into the wind it sails,
Trailing its glossy plumage ruffled, black
Against the lightning glare ; despairing wails
" Kee-ow, t'chuff, t'chuff " the waters echo back.
So desolate and solitary it goes,
Almost extinct, yet proudly carries claws
Of crimson, sickle-curving beak of rose ;
Unknowing follows where death's twilight draws
A beckoning finger, careless of a doom
As sure as that which took our Celtic speech ;
But unforgotten these linked names will loom
In history that time will not outreach.

GLADYS HUNKIN.
Cornish Chough

THREE witches came out of Lundy Cave
Over and under, wave by wave.
Slime and slobber,
Slither and slub,
Over the black rocks
Into the tub.
Out of the black dark
Under the moon
That is the way
Of the witches' rune.
Shriek and scrabble
Scream and shout,
Over and under,
In and out.
The wave comes up
And the witch goes in,
Back to the cauldron
Black as sin !

Shrieking and screaming the white gulls fly
Over the wave where the witches die.
Over and under, wave by wave,
Seaweed twines round the witches' grave.
Green and brown the wet weed flows
—Strands of hair between their toes.

LAWRY HAWKEY.
Lundy Cave

COME on ! come on ! This hillock hides the spire
Now that one and now none. As winds about
The burnished path through lady's-finger, thyme
And bright varieties of saxifrage,
So grows the tinny tenor faint or loud
And all things draw towards St. Enodoc.
Come on ! come on ! and it is five to three.
Paths, unfamiliar to golfers' brogues,
Cross the eleventh fairway broadside on
And leave the fourteenth tee for thirteenth green,
Ignoring Royal and Ancient, bound for God.
Come on ! come on ! no longer bare of foot,
The sole grows hot in London shoes again
Jack Lambourne in his Sunday navy blue
Wears tie and collar, all from Selfridges.
There's Enid with a silly parasol,
And Graham in gray flannel with a crease
Across the middle of his coat which lay
Pressed 'neath the box of his Meccano set,
Sunday to Sunday.
Goes, Come on ! come on !,
The tinny tenor. Hover flies remain
More than a moment on a ragwort bunch,
And peoples' passing shadows don't disturb
Red Admirals basking with their wings apart.

A mile of sunny, empty sand away,
A mile of shallow pools and lugworm casts,
Safe, faint and surfy, beats the lowest tide.
    Even the villas have a Sunday look.
The Ransome mower's locked into the shed
" I have a splitting headache from the sun."
And bedroom windows flutter cheerful chintz
Where double-aspirined, a mother sleeps.
A father in a loggia reads a book,
Large, desultory, birthday-present size,
Published with coloured plates by *Country Life*
A Bernard Darwin on *The English Links*
Or Braid and Taylor on *The Mashie Shot.*
Come on ! come on ! he thinks of Monday's round
Come on ! come on ! that interlocking grip !
Come on ! come on ! he drops into a doze
Come on ! come on ! more far and far away
The children climb a final stile to church.
Electoral Roll still flapping in the porch
Then the cool silence of St. Enodoc.
My eyes, recovering in the sudden shade,
Discern the long-known little things within—
A map of France in damp above my pew,
Grey-blue of granite in the small arcade
(Late Perp. : and not a Parker specimen
But roughly hewn on windy Bodmin Moor)
The modest windows palely glazed with green,
The smooth slate floor, the rounded wooden roof,
The Norman arch, the cable-mounded font,
All have a humble and West Country look.
Oh " drastic restoration " of the guide !
Oh three-light window by a Plymouth firm !
Absurd, truncated screen ! oh sticky pews !
Embroidered altar cloth ! untended lamps !
So soaked in worship you are loved too well
For that dispassionate and critic stare
That I would use beyond the parish bounds
Biking in high-banked lanes from tower to tower
On sunny, antiquarian afternoons.

Come on ! come on ! a final pull. Tom Blake
Slopes over from the bell rope to his pew
In the same manner as he strides the cliffs
Looking for wreckage in a likely tide,
Nor gives the Holy Table glance nor nod.
A rattle as red baize is drawn aside,
Miss Rhoda Poulden pulls the tremolo,
The oboe, flute and vox humana stops :
A Village Voluntary fills the air
And ceases suddenly as it begun,
Save for one oboe faintly humming on,
As slow the weary clergyman subsides
Tired with his bike ride from the parish church.
He runs his hands once, twice, across his face
" Dearly beloved . . ." and a bumble bee
Zooms itself free into the churchyard sun
And so my thoughts this happy Sabbath-tide.
Where deep cliffs loom enormous, where cascade
Mesembryanthemum and stone-crop down,
Where seagulls look no larger than a lark
Hung midway twixt the cliff-top and the sand,
Sun-shadowed valleys roll along the sea.
Forced by the backwash, see the nearest wave
Rise to a wall of huge, translucent green
And crumble into spray along the top
Blown seaward by the landbreeze. Now she breaks
And in an arch of thunder plunges down
To burst and tumble, foam on top of foam,
Criss-crossing, baffled, sucked and shot again
A waterfall of whiteness, down a rock,
Without a source but roller's furthest reach :
And tufts of sea-pink, high and dry for years,
Are flooded out of ledges, boulders seem
No bigger than a pebble washed about
In this tremendous tide. Oh kindly slate !
To give me shelter in this crevice dry.

These shivering stalks of bent-grass, lucky plant,
Have better chance than I to last the storm.
Oh kindly slate of these unaltered cliffs,
Firm, barren substrate of our windy fields !
Oh lichened slate in walls, they knew your worth
Who raised you up to make this House of God
What faith was his, that dim, that Cornish saint,
Small rushlight of a long-forgotten church,
Who lived with God on this unfriendly shore,
Who knew He made the Atlantic and the stones
And destined seamen here to end their lives
Dashed on a rock, rolled over in the surf,
And not one hair forgotten. Now they lie
In centuries of sand beside the church.
Less pitiable are they than the corpse
Of a large golfer, only four weeks dead,
This sunlit and sea-distant afternoon.
" Praise ye the Lord !" and in another key
The Lord's name by harmonium be praised.
" The Second Evening and the Fourteenth Psalm."

> JOHN BETJEMAN.
> *Sunday Afternoon Service in St.*
> *Enodoc Church, Cornwall*

We used to picnic where the thrift
  Grew deep and tufted to the edge ;
We saw the yellow foam-flakes drift
  In trembling sponges on the ledge
Below us, till the wind would lift
  Them up the cliff and o'er the hedge.
    Sand in the sandwiches, wasps in the tea,
    Sun on our bathing dresses heavy with wet,
    Squelch of the bladder wrack waiting for the sea,
    Fleas round the tamarisk, an early cigarette.

From where the coastguard houses stood
  One used to see, below the hill,
The lichened branches of a wood
  In summer silver-cool and still ;
And there the Shade of Evil could
  Stretch out at us from Shilla Mill.
    Thick with sloe and blackberry, uneven in the light,
    Lonely ran the hedge, the heavy meadow was remote,
    The oldest part of Cornwall was the wood as black as night
    And the pheasant and the rabbit lay torn open at the
        throat.

But when a storm was at its height,
  And feathery slate was black in rain,
And tamarisks were hung with light
  And golden sand was brown again,
Spring tide and blizzard would unite
  And sea came flooding up the lane.
    Waves full of treasure then were roaring up the beach
    Ropes round our macintoshes, waders warm and dry,
    We waited for the wreckage to come swirling into reach
    Ralph, Vasey, Alastair, Biddy, John and I.

Then roller into roller curled
  And thundered down the rocky bay,
And we were in a water world
  Of rain and blizzard, sea and spray,
And one against the other hurled
  We struggled round to Greenaway.
    Blessed be St. Enodoc, blessed be the wave
    Blessed be the springy turf, we pray, pray to thee,
    Give to our children all the happy days you gave
    To Ralph, Vasey, Alastair, Biddy, John and me.

JOHN BETJEMAN.
Trebetherick

A flame of rush-light in the cell
On holy walls and holy well
And to the west the thundering bay
With soaking seaweed, sand and spray,

 Oh good St. Cadoc pray for me
 Here in your cell beside the sea.

Somewhere the tree, the yellowing oak,
Is waiting for the woodman's stroke,
Waits for the chisel, saw and plane
To prime it for the earth again.

 And in the earth, for me, inside,
 The generous oak tree will have died.

St. Cadoc blest the woods of oak
Bent landwards by the western lash,
He loved the veined household stones
Where sun might sometime black his bones.

 He had no cowering fear of death
 For breath of God was Cadoc's breath.

Some cavern generates the germs
To send my body to the worms,
To-day some red hands make the shell
To blow my soul away to Hell

 To-day a pair walks newly married
 Along the path where I'll be carried.

St. Cadoc, when the wind was high
Saw angels in the Cornish sky
As ocean rollers curled and poured
Their loud Hosannas to the Lord.

 His little cell was not too small
 For that great Lord who made them all.

Here where St. Cadoc sheltered God
The archaeologist has trod,
Yet death is now the gentle shore
With hand upon the cliffs before
    And in his cell beside the sea
    The Celtic saint has prayed for me.

               JOHN BETJEMAN.
               Saint Cadoc

SIT, with your brown legs dangling,
  Astride the swinging tide ;
Idly the anchored boats sway, and
  Serene the white gulls ride.

Or in the jewelled rock-pool
  Dream out your childhood's day :
Too soon, too soon its morning hours
  Slip soundlessly away.

Cool are those shallows, threading
  Quick eels of sunlight—where
Moored to the limpet-crusted rocks
  Weed drifts like drowned green hair.

That russet sail, ensnaring
  Distance-enchanted eyes,
Haloes the years with promises,
  Beneath unclouded skies.

Tar from coiled rope and baskets
  Piled on this pebbled sand,
Mingles with scorching paint, where boats
  Blister your careless hand

All heedless—unsuspecting
 That life itself may sear
The unwary heart which near the sun
 Soars, ignorant of fear.

How should you guess the quicksands,
 Or hear these small waves sing
Of treacherous currents—how the storm
 Batters the eager wing ;

Of ships in darkness foundering,
 Their voyage scarce begun ? . . .
For you, to-day, the dripping oars
 Flash silver in the sun ;

Blinding your dazzled vision
 To wrack and drifting spars :
Shipwreck's a brave, adventurous word
 To heads among the stars.

The wind on the grey cliff-face
 Rustles the thrift and grass,
Whispering of summer's endless flowers
 (Not that they fade and pass).

So dream, dream on, grave urchin,
 Brim full each wondering sense,
While still you know the untroubled heart,
 The eye of innocence ;

Before the wave engulf you,
 Salt with a cosmic pain,
And these unchanging, timeless sands
 Never be yours again.

MARGARET WILLY.

A Child by the Harbour : Port Isaac
(for Kevin Collins)

TREGEAGLE was a wealthy and powerful man, able, by means of his riches, to keep on the right side both of Church and Law. As a magistrate, he cruelly extinguished those who were offensive to him. His domestic life was diversified by acts of murderous ferocity. As a landlord, his rapacity knew no bounds. When he lay dying, innumerable devils watched expectantly for the flitting soul, but Tregeagle's wealth bought him temporary security, the forces of the Church were marshalled in overwhelming strength, and the body was buried with funeral pomp in the church of St. Breock. Some time after this, a dispute arose concerning the ownership of certain lands near Bodmin. Tregeagle had acted as steward to one of the claimants ; he had forged documents, transferred deeds illegally, and brought affairs into a pretty pass. At the final hearing of the case, the defendant asked leave to produce an additional witness. The witness entered the court, and was recognized as Tregeagle himself, pale and terrible, raised from the dead. The examination of this ghastly witness revealed the true facts of the case, and the defendant proved his right to the land. But Tregeagle had to be disposed of, and the defendant, observing that he entrusted him to the care of the Judge and the Prior with whom he had been on such excellent terms, walked out of the court. And now a sickening, chill horror filled the room, while priests and lawyers wrangled and reasoned and Tregeagle stood there in silence. It was decided that he should be taken to Dosmary Pool, protected by holy spells, and set to work to bale out the water with a perforated limpet shell. This was done ; but the devils, not despairing of their dues, kept incessant watch on the wretched creature, seeking to drive him from his task and into their clutches. So they raised a terrible storm, and Tregeagle, smitten by icy hails, scorched by lightnings, bent in the blast of the tempest, fled from the pool. At his heels ran a legion of bellowing demons, and thrice round the pool raced dead man and devils, with such cries and roarings, all mixed with the fury of the storm, that any man who heard them would have gone stark raving mad. After the third round, Tregeagle, endowed with miraculous strength and lightness, leapt clean across the water, and rushed over the moors to the holy oratory of St. Roche. Up the rock he flew, and pushed his head in through the window, to the dismay of the good hermit, and there he stuck. There he stuck for days ; convulsed with the agonies of the damned every time the saint said his prayers, and driving away all the devout folk from the chapel. But he dared not back out, for the devils hovered in the wind to take him.

St. Roche, as you can imagine, realizing that there are limits even to the hospitality of a sanctuary, was anxious to get rid of his visitor. He mustered a strong force of holy men, and Tregeagle was escorted to Padstow, where he was set to weave ropes of sand. Here, his direful howling annoyed the people, who applied to St. Petroc for assistance. Petroc bound Tregeagle with mystical fetters and took him to Berepper, about two miles south of Helston, where he was given the task of carrying sacks of sand across the Loo estuary and emptying them at Porth Leven. Roaring like a bull, he toiled industriously, but one day the devil tripped him up and he sprawled into the sea, scattering his load of sand. This sand may yet be seen ; it is known as Loo Bar, and it blocks the sea-approach to Helston. The people of Helston, who found their place converted by this sudden accident from a flourishing port to an inland village, and who were, moreover, sadly disturbed by the roaring of Tregeagle, told the holy men plainly that they must make other arrangements. By the power of holy enchantments Tregeagle was conveyed to the Land's End. There he was employed in sweeping the sand from Porthcurno round Tol-Pedn into Nanjizal Bay, and there he is still at work. On stormy nights you will hear the tortured Tregeagle, now screaming, now roaring ; Tregeagle outcast, neither saved nor yet wholly damned ; devoted eternally to a hopeless task, a lonely and a furious ghost—" Tregeagle the Bull."

C. E. VULLIAMY.

The Legend of Tregeagle

H

DESOLATE that cry as though world were unworthy.
See now, rounding the headland, a forlorn hopeless bird,
trembling black wings, fingering the blowy air,
dainty and ghostly, careless of the scattering salt.

This is the cave-dweller that flies like a butterfly,
buffeted by daws, almost extinct, who has chosen,
so gentle a bird, to live on furious coasts.

Here where sea whistles in funnels, and slaps the back
of burly granite slabs, and hisses over holes,
in bellowing hollows that shelter the female seal
the Cornish chough wavers over the waters.
By lion rocks, rocks like the heads of queens,
sailing with ragged plumes upturned, into the wind
goes delicate indifferent the doomed bird.

REX WARNER.
Chough

FROM out the wood I watched them shine,
    The windows of the haunted house,
Now ruddy as enchanted wine,
    Now dark as flittermouse.

There went a thin voice piping airs
    Along the grey and crooked walks,
A garden of thistledown and tares,
    Bright leaves and giant stalks.

The twilight rain shone at its gates,
    Where long-leaved grass in shadow grew ;
And back in silence to her mates
    A voiceless raven flew.

Lichen and moss the lone stones greened,
   Green paths led lightly to its door,
Keen from her lair the spider leaned,
   And dusk to darkness wore.

Amidst the sedge a whisper ran,
   The west shut down a heavy eye,
And like last tapers, few and wan,
   The watch-stars kindled in the sky.

WALTER DE LA MARE.
Haunted

" THE valley of the river Camel is full of haunted lanes and
houses. A mile or so up the river stands the ancient church of
Egloshayle. Under a night-sky the church is scarcely visible.
But if the clouds roll back from the moon, and let a sudden
blaze of light fall over the river bed, you will see the old gray
tower clearly, standing out from a group of chestnut trees,
and may even discern an open space beside the churchyard
wall where the high-road meets the lane leading to the village.
The road gleams beneath the moonlight ; but you are too far
distant to see any object moving on it.

   If it were otherwise, you might now see—but never save
when the moon is bright—a white rabbit gambolling about
this open space beside the churchyard wall ; a pretty, long-
eared rabbit with pink eyes, like any child's pet escaped from
its hutch. It goes loppeting about among the grasses by the
corner of the marsh ; and if anyone should pass, will sit and
look at him with fearless eyes. And well it may be. It has
nothing to dread from any one dwelling in those parts. No
villager would attempt to catch it. No boy would aim a blow
at it. If any one walking late sees the white rabbit lopping
at his heels, he makes no effort to drive it away, but quickens
his pace, and hopes some good angel may stand between him
and harm. A belated postman, terrified to find he could not
hake off the pretty creature at his heels, lost his head and

turned and struck fiercely at it with his oaken cudgel. He felt
the stick fall on the soft back of the rabbit, such a blow as
might have killed a much larger animal. But the rabbit lopped
on as if nothing had happened. The cudgel it was which was
broken—shivered into splinters, as if it had struck upon a
rock . . .

No one can tell the history of the rabbit; but our grand-
fathers knew and feared it as we do ourselves."

ARTHUR H. NORWAY.
The White Rabbit of Egloshayle

COME all you jovial ringers,
   Come listen to my tale;
I'll tell you of five Ringers bold
   That liv'd in Egloshayle—
For ring the ray they bore the sway
   Wherever they did go;
The music of the merry bells
   'Twas their delight to show.

There was Craddock the Cordwinder,
   He ring the Treble Bell;
John Ellery was the second man,
   And few could him excel.
The third was Pollard the Carpenter,
   And the fourth was Thomas Cleave,
And Goodfellow the Tenor man,
   That rung him round so brave.

Now Craddock was the Treble man;
   He stepped 'long with his toe,
And casting of his eyes around,
   Commanded them when to go.
They pulled away with courage bold,
   Which did their hearts revive;
Sweet music then was quickly heard,
   (With) " one, two, three, four, five !"

They went out to Lanlivery ;
   They brought away the prize.
They came back to St. Tudy,
   And done the same likewise.
There was Lanlivery men, St. Mabyn men,
   St. Tudy and St. Kew—
But those five lads of Egloshayle
   Did all the rest outdo.

*This little core,** they play'd so sure,
   No changes did they fear ;
No man did ever miss his turn—
   'Twas joy to see and hear !
And people all, for miles around,
   Did tell o'er hill and dale
The fame of those five Ringers bold
   That liv'd in Egloshayle.

TRADITIONAL
The Ringers of Egloshayle

" Next, I will relate you another of the *Cornish* natural wonders,
viz. S. *Kaynes* well : but lest you make a worder first at the
Saint, before you take notice of the well, you must understand,
that this was not *Kayne* the man-queller, but one of a gentler
spirit, and milder sex, to wit a woman. He who caused the
spring to be pictured, added this rime for an exposition :—

In name, in shape, in quality,
   The well is very quaint ;
The name to lot of Kayne befell,
   No ower-holy saint.
The shape—four trees of divers kinds,
   Withy, oke, elme and ash,

* This verse has been reconstructed from fragments.
** Corps

Make with their roots an arched roofe,
  Whose floore this spring doth wash.
The quality—that man or wife,
  Whose chance or choice attaines,
First of the sacred stream to drinke,
  Thereby the mastry gaines."

RICHARD CAREW, 1602.
The Well of St. Keyne
From " *The Survey of Cornwall* "

I know not whether it be worth reporting, that there is in
Cornwall, near the parish of St. Neots, a well arched over
with the robes of four kinds of trees, withy, oak, elm and ash,
dedicated to St. Keyne. The reported virtue of the water is
this, that whether husband or wife come first to drink thereof,
they get the mastery thereby.

FULLER.

A well there is in the west country,
  And a clearer one never was seen ;
There is not a wife in the west-country
  But has heard of the well of St. Keyne.

An oak and an elm tree stand beside,
  And behind does an ash tree grow,
And a willow from the bank above
  Droops to the water below.

A traveller came to the Well of St. Keyne ;
  Pleasant it was to his eye,
For from cock-crow he had been travelling
  And there was not a cloud in the sky.

He drank of the water so cool and clear,
   For thirsty and hot was he,
And he sat down upon the bank,
   Under the willow tree.

There came a man from the neighbouring town
   At the well to fill his pail,
On the well-side he rested it,
   And bade the stranger hail.

Now art though a bachelor, stranger ? quoth he,
   For an if thou hast a wife,
The happiest draught thou hast drunk this day
   That ever thou didst in thy life.

Or has your good woman, if you have one,
   In Cornwall ever been ?
For an if she have, I'll venture my life
   She has drunk of the well of St. Keyne.

I have left a good woman who never was here,
   The stranger he made reply ;
But that my draught should be better for that,
   I pray you answer me why.

St. Keyne, quoth the countryman, many a time
   Drank of this crystal well,
And before the angel summoned her
   She laid on the water a spell.

If the husband of this gifted well
   Shall drink before his wife,
A happy man henceforth is he,
   For he shall be master for life.

But if the wife should drink of it first,
   God help the husband then !
The stranger stoop'd to the well of St. Keyne,
   And drank of the waters again,

You drank of the well, I warrant, betimes ?
    He to the countryman said.
But the countryman smiled as the stranger spake,
    And sheepishly shook his head.

I hasten'd as soon as the wedding was done,
    And left my wife in the porch.
But i' faith she had been wiser than me,
    For she took a bottle to church.

ROBERT SOUTHEY.
The Well of St. Keyne

SITTING in the firelight's glow—
How do we know
What is blowing in the wind outside,
What is riding on the dark hillside,
Who is moaning under the stair,
What is burning in the red flame's glare ?
And where, where
Are the white ghosts riding ?
Who, who is the spectre chiding ?
Can we know what listens at the dark key-hole ?
Can we feel what clutches at the edge of the soul ?
Whence come the thoughts that are flaming and growing ?
Who planted the seeds and when was the sowing ?
Alas and alack there is no knowing.

LAWRY HAWKEY.
Jamaica Inn

LESS vast, less lofty than the moors of Devon, but infinitely more mysterious, more varied in form and mood, the Cornish moors have a penetrating charm which is peculiar to themselves. In all their aspects they have a strange, almost a menacing beauty ; something that eludes all wordy striving ; mutable yet eternal, transient as the shadow of a cloud, yet steadfast as the granite on their brows. On these airy downs and uplands you will find Unknown Cornwall. You find an exalted liberty, a sense of the timeless youth of the world, of the fervour and fertility of nature ; you apprehend, dimly, a new, inexpressible and joyous dimension. The very air has a kind of unearthly purity, thinness and fragrance, blowing free under the clean, open heavens, and stirring the scents of furze-bloom and bracken. No one can say that he knows the moors, that they have no revelations in store for him, that he is intimate with all their deep and bountiful beauties, has read their meaning, disclosed all their sweetness and terror—or if anyone should so speak, then he would make it clear that he had neither eyes to see nor a spirit to apprehend.

Such is the strange power and allurement of the moors that the most portly and torpid persons become infected thereby ; and I have seen old gentlemen conduct themselves, when actuated by these strange yet impalpable influences, in a very surprising and extravagant manner. The man who could walk the moors in undeviating, unwondering stolidity would be altogether outside my sympathy or comprehension. I should be astonished if the most forlorn, bespatted and tremulously respectable old city drudge failed to brighten up and enjoy the pleasure of living when he found himself on these moors. As for you and me, we are no sooner joyously unloosed on the uplands—why, all our cares and woes, straightway fall from us with as sudden and gladsome a thump as the Pilgrim's packet of sins ; the blessed air of Cornwall fills our lungs, tingling and stinging blithely like bumpers of heady wine ; before our eyes the wonderful, billowy line of the hills rolls in grand and gracious curves towards the valleys and the sea.

C. E. VULLIAMY.
The Cornish Moors

On ancient roads our fathers made
    By seaboard hill and moor,
We follow in their footsteps still
    To mine and farm and shore.
And where they passed they left behind
    Their music by the way
In ancient names that in our ears
    Are ringing still to-day.

Tre, Ros, Pol, Lan, Car, Tol, Pen,
Ring a peal to Cornishmen.

On moor and hill our fathers left
    Their monuments in stone
To tell of bygone mysteries,
    A heritage we own.
In mystic circles we may know
    Dividing Time to cease,
And still may hear the ancient call
    And join the cry for ' Peace.'

Dâwns Men, Hurlers, Boscawen-Un,
Echo still an ancient tune.

In far-off days our fathers fought
    Invading hordes to stay ;
In living legends they endure,
    Their cromlechs stand to-day.
Great Arthur's spirit potent still,
    Feeds an undying fire ;
Still gleams the brand Excalibur
    To beacon and inspire.

Arthur, Galahad, Bedivere,
Cornishmen their call can hear.

In ancient days when Saints had come
    To dwell by well and spring,
Our fathers raised their crosses high
    A sign for worshipping.
Then churches rose with stately towers,
    And bells their pride to crown.
And now the tide of music flows
    From Rame to Sennen Town.

Truro, Bodmin, Padstow, Paul,
Ring their chimes to One and All.

BERNARD MOORE.
A Song for Cornwall

WHEN Sir Jonathan Trelawny, one of the Seven Bishops, was committed to the Tower, the Cornish Men rose one and all and marched as far as Exeter on their way to extort his liberation.

A good sword and a trusty hand !
    A merry heart and true !
King James's men shall understand
    What Cornish lads can do !

And have they fixed the where and when ?
    And shall Trelawny die ?
Here's twenty thousand Cornish men
    Will see the reason why.

Out spake their Captain brave and bold
    A merry wight was he
" If London Tower were Michael's hold
    We'll set Trelawny free !

We'll cross the Tamar, land to land,
   The Severn is no stay—
And side by side, and hand to hand,
   And who shall bid us nay !

And when we come to London Wall
   A pleasant sight to view,
Come forth ! come forth ! ye cowards all
   To better men than you !

Trelawny's he's in keep and hold,
   Trelawny he may die,
But here's twenty thousand Cornish bold
   Will see the reason why !

R. S. HAWKER, 1825.
The Song of the Western Men

WE who were born in this sea-bound peninsula,
With salt on our lips and brine for blood,
Love the variety steadfast in change,
The ceaseless murmuration of the sea ;
Where it curdles in cauldrons, seethes over boulders,
Reverberates through caves in granite and serpentine
Beats on resistant piled stacks of rock—
Armed Knight and Shark's Fin and Samphire Island,
Thunders round Dodman and roars on Doom Bar ;
Foams epileptically over fanged Manacles,
Gloating on wrecks, heaving ashore soaked corpses,
Knotted cordage and spars as spent matchwood ;

Slaps the shelved slate at Boscastle ;
The slow, heavy, oiled mass of the long roller
Breaks in a resonant crash ;
Heaps waves again one after one till the ninth
Sends screaming the foam-light sea-gull,
But leaves unperturbed the cormorant,
Breasting the breaker and ready to dive
In its concave trough, missing death by a fragment.
Spues from currents and moon-pulled tides,
Wide ribboned strands of brown storm-wrack.
The wind shrieks—" To-morrow, to-morrow,"
A promised release, with tempest subsiding—
Then the sea in a mood of smiling demeanour,
Sweeps through tidal estuaries, sidles in creeks,
Lap-laps the posts and stone steps of the quays,
Floods the safe harbour of Falmouth
Where the great ships ride at anchor.
Lips the chrome sand of the quiet coves,
Purling on pebbles, ebbing from rock pools
Where we lazily dabbled an arm to the shoulder.
Cold itself, clasps the cool moon to its bosom,
Scatters a sprinkling of powdered stars,
Reflects fanned lights of light-houses and ships,
Gathers the topaz flecks of the sun
And shakes them as gems in a jade green bowl.
Long days we've lain in the ling and bracken,
Wrapped in its scent and the tang of the spray,
Above rippled stretches of jaspé satin,
League upon league the illimitable sea.

GLADYS HUNKIN.
The Sea

Arise ! and away ! for the King and the land ;
  Farewell to the couch and the pillow :
With spear in the rest, and with rein in the hand,
  Let us rush on the foe like a billow.

Call the hind from the plough, and the herd from the fold
  Bid the wassailer cease from his revel :
And ride for old Stowe ; where the banner's unrolled,
  For the cause of King Charles and Sir Beville.

Trevanion is up, and Godolphin is nigh,
  And Harris of Hayne's o'er the river :
From Lundy to Looe, " One and all !" is the cry,
  And the King and Sir Beville for ever !

Ay, by Tre, Pol and Pen, ye may know Cornishmen,
  'Mid the names and the nobles of Devon ;
But if truth to the King be a signal, why then
  Ye can find out the Granville in heaven.

Ride ! ride ! with red spur, there is death in delay,
  'Tis a race for dear life with the devil ;
If dark Cromwell prevail, and the King must give way,
  This earth is no place for Sir Beville.

So at Stamford he fought, and at Lansdowne he fell,
  But in vain were the visions he cherished . . .
For the great Cornish heart, that the King loved so well,
  In the grave of the Granville it perished.

R. S. HAWKER.
Sir Beville—The Gate-song of Stowe

Iseult, Iseult, by the long waterways
Watching the wintry moon, white as a flower,
I have remembered how once in Tintagil
You heard the breath of Time, hour after hour.

By casement hung with night, while all your women slept
You turned toward Brittany, awake, alone,
In the high chamber hushed, save where the candle dripped
With the slow patient sound of blood on stone.

The ache of empty arms was an old tale to you,
And all the tragic tunes that love can play,
Yet with no woman born would you have changed your lot,
Though there were greater queens who had been gay.

SARA TEASDALE.
At Tintagil

There stands a headland by the Western shore
    Dreamy and dark ; half-cloven from the land
    By old upheaval, or Time's gradual hand.
The broad Atlantic rolls from Labrador,
With slow, long-heaving, untumultuous roar,
    His serried legions on th' embattled coast.
    But vain the onset of the billowy host :
King Arthur guards his hold for evermore.

Tintagel ! fallen are thy towers to-day :
    A little postern in a crumbled wall,
    Gain'd by a perilous pathway ; this is all
Time spares from desolation and decay.
Yet are thy ruins, long as time shall last,
Builded with visions of the phantom past.

C. E. BYLES.
Tintagel

NATURE to famed Tintagel yields a glory
   In cliffs stupendous breasting ocean's roar ;
Cliffs, strong-armed giants ages have made hoary,
   Guarding wild Cornwall's shore.

History and legend make the spot around us
   Immortal, though dumb Solitude sits queen :
A chain of interest and deep awe hath bound us,
   Enchantment fills the scene.

Here while we listen to the billows' thunder,
   Waves tossing, rolling in their mad unrest,
Spray, like broad sheets of snow, a whitening wonder,
   Flung up from ocean's breast :

Fancy will see King Arthur's ghost lone standing,
   Misty, gigantic, on yon beetling rock,
All cased in steel, as if some host commanding,
   Waiting the battle's shock.

We see him now, his skeleton arms extending
   To where his castle stood, high-walled and strong,
Back over days of splendour, memory sending—
   Days of pomp, feast and song.

He hears, upon the landward breezes swelling,
   The shouts of heroes, woman's laughter sweet—
All of his once-loved Cornish kingdom telling ;
   His knights he seems to greet.

Poor ghost ! he vanishes mid foam of ocean,
   His glittering mail, sword, spear, have passed away ;
The tufted sea-pink, with a tremulous motion,
   Waves on his castle grey.

Bald stones his once grand fortress—let us listen !
   For battle shouts and songs of ladies fair,
We hear the cormorant's cry where wet rocks glisten,
   And seaweeds trail their hair.

In tiltyard and grassed keep the rabbits burrow,
    And, mid the wild flowers, hums the reckless drone ;
Below, the waves, in chasms and long furrows,
    Wear rocks, and dash and moan.

Grim Ruin folds her mantle, pensive sitting
    By crumbled walls ; she cries " The scene is mine !"
There Desolation's shade is nightly flitting,
    Shrieking, as moonbeams shine.

Yes, as the wan, pure light around is falling,
    Silvering the crags and ocean's tossing spray,
A voice from out the mouldered stones seems calling,
    " Thus pomp, power, melt away !"

Yet down the ages, O ye Rocks and Ocean !
    When cold this heart, and dim this raptured eye,
Pilgrims will seek your shore in warm devotion,
    Pondering on years gone by.

When not a stone of Arthur's pile is frowning
    Above the waste of thundering waves below,
Song with its magic will these cliffs be crowning,
    Brightening the long ago :

'Gainst desolate rocks the billows will be dashing,
    But fancy shall place form on crag and hill ;
And warm Romance, her bright eyes backward flashing,
    Halo Tintagel still.

NICHOLAS MICHELL.
Tintagel

". . . High into the morning sprang,
Riven from the shore and bastioned with the sea,
Toward summits where the north wind's nest might be,
A wave-walled palace with its eastern gate
Full of the sunrise now and wide at wait,
And on the mighty-moulded stairs that clomb
Sheer from the fierce lip of the lapping foam
The knights of Mark that stood before the wall.
So with loud joy and storm of festival
They brought the bride in up the towery way
That rose against the rising front of day,
Stair based on stair, between the rocks unhewn,
To those strange halls where through the tidal tune
Rang loud or lower from soft or strengthening sea,
Tower shouldering tower, to windward and to lee,
With change of floors and stories, flight on flight,
That clomb and curled up to the crowning height
Whence men might see wide east and west in one
And on one sea waned moon and mounting sun.
And severed from the sea-rock's base, where stand
Some worn walls yet they saw the broken strand,
The beachless cliff that in the sheer sea dips,
The sleepless shore inexorable to ships,
And the straight causeway's bare gaunt spine between
The sea-spanned walls and naked mainland's green."

ALGERNON CHARLES SWINBURNE.
From "*Tristram of Lyonesse*"

The year lies fallen and faded
On cliffs by clouds invaded,
With tongues of storms upbraided,
        With wrath of waves bedinned.
And inland, wild with warning,
As in deaf ears or scorning,
The clarion even and morning
        Rings of the south-west wind.

The wild bents wane and wither
In blasts whose breath bows hither
Their grey-grown heads and thither,
    Unblest of rain or sun ;
The pale fierce heavens are crowded
With shapes like dreams beclouded,
As though the old year enshrouded
    Lay, long ere life were done.

Full-charged with old-world wonders,
From dusk Tintagel thunders
A note that smites and sunders
    The hard frore fields of air ;
A trumpet stormier-sounded
Than once from lists rebounded
When strong men sense-confounded
    Fell thick in tourney there.

From scarce a duskier dwelling
Such notes of wait rose welling
Through the outer darkness, telling
    In the awful singer's ears
What souls the darkness covers,
What love-lost soul of lovers,
Whose cry still hangs and hovers
    In each man's born that hears.

For there by Hector's brother
And yet some thousand other
He that had grief to mother
    Passed pale from Dante's sight ;
With one fast linked as fearless,
Perchance, there only tearless ;
Iseult and Tristram, peerless
    And perfect queen and knight.

A shrill-winged sound comes flying
North, as of wild souls crying
The cry of things undying,
    That know what life must be ;
Or as the old year's hear, stricken
Too sore for hope to quicken
By thought like thorns that thicken,
    Broke, breaking with the sea.

A. C. SWINBURNE.
Autumn in Cornwall

I found her out there
On a slope few see,
That falls westwardly
To the salt-edged air,
Where the ocean breaks
On the purple strand,
And the hurricane shakes
The solid land.

I brought her here,
And have laid her to rest
In a noiseless nest
No sea beats near.
She will never be stirred
In her loamy cell
By the waves long heard
And loved so well.

So she does not sleep
By those haunted heights
The Atlantic strikes
And the blind gales sweep,
Whence she often would gaze
At Dundagel's famed head,
While the dipping blaze
Dyed her face fire-red ;

And would sigh at the tale
Of sunk Lyonnesse,
As a wind-tugged tress
Flapped her cheek like a flail ;
Or listen at whiles
With a thought-bound brow
To the murmuring miles
She is far from now.

Yet her shade, maybe,
Will creep underground
Till it catch the sound
Of that western sea
As it swells and sobs
Where she once domiciled,
And joy in its throbs
With the heart of a child.

THOMAS HARDY.
I Found Her Out There

I

O the opal and the sapphire of that wandering western sea,
And the woman riding high above with bright hair flapping
   free—
The woman whom I loved so, and who loyally loved me.

II

The pale mews plained below us, and the waves seemed far
   away
In a nether sky, engrossed in saying their ceaseless babbling
   say,
As we laughed light-heartedly aloft on that clear-sunned
   March day.

III

A little cloud then cloaked us, and there flew an irised rain,
And the Atlantic dyed its levels with a dull mis-featured stain,
And then the sun burst out again, and purples prinked the
   main.

IV

—Still in all its chasmal beauty bulks old Beeny to the sky,
And shall she and I not go there once again now March is
   nigh
And the sweet things said in that March say anew there by
   and by ?

V

What if still in chasmal beauty looms that wild weird western
   shore,
The woman now is—elsewhere—whom the ambling pony bore,
And nor knows nor cares for Beeny, and will laugh there
   nevermore.

THOMAS HARDY.
Beeny Cliff

FROM Cumberland my fathers came,
   my mothers, from the west ;
   and each in turn, at fitting time,
   I choose to love as best ;

for Patterdale is very strong,
   and strength belongs to gaunt Scaw Fell,
   and in the west, as well I know,
   the moor is strong on Bodmin heights.

No wonder, when the snow has come,
I look to crag and fell,
and in the spring I know my home
lies in a Cornish dell.

Had I to choose to have or lose
the stalwart north, the willing west,
then—saddened that they cannot fuse—
I own I'd take the west as best.

J. H. B. PEEL.
North and West

I WILL sing a song of love,
and my adoration prove
for the beauty of the sky
burnished flawless through July.
I will sing a song of pleasure
that the gods ordained me leisure
to enjoy the fullest measure
of this island trove of treasure.
I will make a thing of joy
from delights that never cloy.
I will praise the little things
—dandelions, and fishes' rings
cooing silent on a stream
where the midges whirl and dream.
I will sing the things that move
—sun ascending in a groove
carved by beauty on the sky,
doomed each day to live and die.
I will sing the things that stand
hills and trees and Cornish sand.
I will make a lover's chain
blent of visitors—the rain,
snow, and cuckoo in the copse,
cherry blossom, harvest crops.

I will sing of sojourners
lovelier than visitors
—robin steadfast through the year,
lovers young or in the sere,
inn-sign swinging from its rafter,
birth and death and present laughter.

J. H. B. PEEL.
Love Poem

SEPTEMBER wanes. Dew-pearled silk webs conceal
    The spiky branches of the dusky thorn.
Dark ships at sunrise from the harbour steal,
    Like shadows, through the golden mist of dawn.

Sharp winds and rain have stripped the trembling trees,
    From every twig the faded leaves are torn,
But where they died, behold, the green buds grow.
    In the first hour of Autumn Spring is born.

A.S.
Autumn in Cornwall

" CORNWALL is incomparably the strangest, most alluring and
most wonderful of all the counties of England. In Cornwall
there is a mystic interfusion of past and present, of the new
and ancient, which is not suggested in many other places,
even where the wrecks of antiquity dominate in every sense
of the word. I have felt such a sensation in looking from the

tumbled walls of Troy, across the Plain and across the Straits
to where the hollow hull of the ' River Clyde,' just discernible,
stood below the ruins of Sedd-ul-Bahr. It is a sensation in
which the illusion of time becomes momentarily apparent ;
in which the imaginery division between past and present is
dissolved, and we are as conscious of the verity of the one as
of the other. Looking from the hill of Hissarlik towards that
yellow shore with its ruined forts, it may have been some
recognition of the fellowship in great deeds of arms between
the fighters of the Trojan wars and those who ran against the
machine guns on that ghastly beach, some sense of the link
between old tradition and modern daring, which gave a kind
of immediacy to the acts of the past and induced a refluence
of what we term the actual. The two concepts merged into
each other. That is what you feel in the old stone enclosures
of the Cornish moors, in the abandoned primitive villages and
in the circles. Time suffers a contraction : you realize that
you are close to the ancient builders, that the ' o'd people '
have left behind them, in these stones, something of themselves
which is not only living but cognizant, and not only cognizant
but definitely friendly or hostile. I have seen vaster ruins in
wilder places, but I have never felt the same intimacy with
the primitive and prehistoric that I have felt in Cornwall.
Neither is this sensation peculiar to myself. It is felt by
everyone who gets into touch with the true character of that
marvellous land, even by those who are unversed alike in
legend and in learning.

Thus, Cornwall has a life, an existence, a meaning, apart
altogether from the fretting cares and dissolving joys of the
present. Therein lies her charm, her power to enslave or
distract, her call, and, to some, her terrors.

Mysterious land ! Even to those who are familiar with
her moods and appearances and with all the features of her
coast and landscape she remains, in the profounder sense,
Unknown Cornwall.

C. E. VULLIAMY.
From *"Unknown Cornwall"*

LORD of all lands, our songs of praise
With thankful hearts to Thee we raise,
And more because Thy kindly hand
Has given us this, our native land.

Lord of the sea that guards our shore
And feeds us with unfailing store,
Great Ruler of its majesty,
We thank Thee for Thy gift, the sea.

Lord of the earth whose deeps enfold
A wondrous store of wealth untold,
That we may use and have no dearth,
We thank Thee for Thy generous earth.

Lord of the sky that sends the rain
To tend our fields for fruit and grain,
And sun, to bring the harvest high,
We thank Thee for Thy sun and sky.

Great Lord of ALL, enthroned above,
We know Thy pity, and Thy love ;
Thy grace shall save us when we fall,
And guard and guide us, ONE and ALL.

BERNARD MOORE.
Cornish Hymn
Our Native Land

ARLUTH pup tyr, y-grassyn Dhys
A'n da a-wreth a 'gan govys,
Dres oll dre wul a'th torn dyghow
An tyr dhyn us mar ger, Kernow.

Arluth an mor, a-wyth hy als
Hag a-gan-mak gans puscas pals,
Penvyghtern war y fas hep for',
Gras a-aswonyn Dhys a'n mor.

Arluth an dor, us yn y gres
Cober ha sten rag agan les,
Hep fyllel dhyn ow-ry tresor,
Gras a-aswonyn Dhys a'n dor.

Arluth an nef, ow-ry an glaw
Frut agan lafur-oll a-saw,
Ha'n howl, dhyn trevas hel a-sef,
Gras a-aswonyn Dhys a'n nef.

Arluth Pup-oll, avan y'th tron,
Dha dhader mur ny a-n-aswon ;
Dha drueth a-gan-gwyth rag coll,
Ha'th gras a-led Onen hag Oll.

Hympna Kernow
(Translated into Cornish by R. Morton Nance)
Agan Tyr Genesyk

O merry ring the Christmas bells
    across the Western land,
From Launceston town to Michael's Mount,
    from Bude to Sennen Sand.
The joyous echo sweeps along
    far spaces by the sea,
And Church bells answer Church bells with
    their ' Gloria, Domine !'

    O Cornish bells, ring far, ring free,
    Ring—' Gloria tibi, Domine !'

High o'er the ridge of Bodmin moor
    grey Rowtor keepeth guard,
His age-worn crown of granite crag
    by wind and storm is scarred.
But here as once in Bethlehem
    the Christmas stars shine bright,
And moorland men are wending far
    to Church on Christmas night.

O Bodmin bells, ring far, ring free,

O hark the bells of Liskeard how
    they call the bells of Looe,
S. Winnow and Lansallos
    Lostwithiel and Duloe,
Till all the upland pulses with
    the Glorious Hymn of Joy,
As Talland calls to Lanreath and
    Lanteglos answers Fowey.

O Liskeard bells, ring far, ring free,

O'er Mordred's town, by Michael's rock, the
    bells of Roche out-tell
Their silver call to Wenna's fane beyond
    the Holy Well :
O ! Columb's Hill ; O ! Deny's heights,
    the gladsome chorus sing,
Till all Luxulyan's rock-piled dells
    with clashing echoes ring.

O Roche Church bells, ring far, ring free,

Ring gladsome bells, ring pealing bells
    from Falmouth harbour wide,
To where S. Mary's Minster stands
    above the Truro tide.

Ring Christmas bells of Roseland
    in your maddest merriest glee,
From Probus to Penkevil,
    from Lamorran to the sea.

      O Kenwyn bells, ring far, ring free,

As by the mystic star of old
    the Magian kings were led,
So homing boats on Christmas Eve
    by lights of Lizard Head ;
And fisher lads safe home at last
    from peril on the sea,
Give incense of brave hearts to greet
    their Lord's Epiphany.

      O Keverne bells, ring far, riug free,

Round dark Tintagel's castled crag,
    round Gurnard's Titan keep,
The long Atlantic rollers boom
    their organ-music deep,
And Buryan bells o'er land and sea
    the Christmas message bear
To where the dreaming Scillies sleep
    in moon-enchanted air.

      O Buryan bells, ring far, ring free,

O magic moon ! O mystic stars !
    O music of the night !
Your ' Gloria in Excelsis ' sing,
    O Praise Him in the Height !

' On earth be Peace, Good-will to men !'
    it is the Angel's song—
Ring Cornish bells, ring one and all,
    come sweep the Hymn along !

Ring Cornish bells oe'r land and sea,

BISHOP C. W. STUBBS.
The Cornish Bells

THE old sea here at my door
    The old hills there in the West—
What can a man want more
    Till he goes at last to his rest ?

I have wandered over the earth,
    I have lived in the years gone by.
Now here, in the place of my birth,
    I wait till 'tis time to die :

To sleep and to take my rest,
    The old sea here at my door,
The grey hills there in the West . . .
    What can a man want more ?

H. D. LOWRY.

" YES, a magpie on a wind-clipt thorn bush, a yellow-hammer
on a furze spray, gulls behind a ploughshare, a cormorant on
a rock in the green water, and jack-daws about a broken
mine-stack, are pictures downright Cornish ; and they are
always with us."

J. C. TREGARTHEN.
Downright Cornish

THE mine stacks spire around Redruth
   And mark the slopes to Camborne Town,
While high above, grim sentinel
   Carn Brea looks down.
Through hump-backed hills the reddened streams
   Babble their journey to the sea
By valleys flanked with gorse and heath
   And briony.
On wind-swept heights, in lowly vales,
   Old churches raise their towers, and tell
The history of ancient days
   In book and bell,
And as we view our Cornish scene
   We know that there are other eyes
That picture it from far away
   'Neath alien skies.
Eyes that from pitted lands look out
   Across the ocean wild and wide
And catch the sun on Illogan
   At eventide
And eyes beneath the Southern Cross
   That look from half the world away
To autumn moorland bracken-brown
   And granite-grey
They gaze on winding hillside roads
   Dear in the ward of memory ;
They see the valleyed ways that turn
   Down to the sea.
And through the clamour of the stamps
   A far off music breaks and swells,
The murmuring of reddened streams,
   And old Church bells,
The little Bethel's hymns of praise,
   The trumpeting of village bands,
The gale brought breakers when they roar
   On Portreath sands.
Malaya—Michigan—Peru—
   Wherever Cornishmen may roam

They take with them the sounds, the scenes
   The thoughts of home.
They tread in memory the roads
   Around Redruth and Camborne Town
Where high above—grim sentinel,
   Carn Brea looks down.

BERNARD MOORE.
Homeways

FROM Ghoulies and Ghosties
and long leggety Beasties
and all Things that gang
bump in the night—
   Good Lord deliver us !

TRADITIONAL
Old Cornish Litany

ST. DOMINIC, TAMAR VALLEY

" . . . Tranquillity
is woven with the whiteness of the
blossom
and waits all softly on a western
sky."

J. H. B. PEEL

Photo : " The Times "

COTEHELE HOUSE

" Firm stands its grey embattled wall,
The rusted armour crowds the hall,
And the queer carven furniture
Doth still the worm's slow tooth endure :
The storied tapestry still hangs,
Scarce injured by the moths' keen fangs ;
And on the stout limb'd board remain
The cups our fathers loved to drain."

H. SEWELL STOKES

Photo : Muriel Hawkey

COTTAGE IN TAMAR VALLEY

" Low in the valley's cup
  Brimmed by green hills,
Where the shining Tamar
  Winds as it wills,
In a hushed garden
  Memories unfold,
Stands a lone cottage
  Growing gently old."   MARY VOSPER PRIOR

Photo : Fox Photos Ltd

" The sound of water . . .
Falling through the woods,
Making more solitary
The ancient solitudes."

A. L. ROWSE

" Midstream the circling ripples slowly
      ebb,
Change to a green stillness, reflect,
      display
A passing bird, trees at the river's
      edge,
The quiet sky and the twilight end
      of day."

                A.S.

Photo : Frank Grattan, A.R.P.

" That haunt of peace, that valley fair
Shows but the change the seasons bring,
The flowery cycle of the year."

MARGARET BONE

Photo : *Frank Grattan, A.R.P.S.*

" . . . The sea swung by
Dazzling dark blue and verduous, quiet
with snow,
Empty with loveliness, with music a-roar,
Her billowing summits heaving noon-aglow—
Crashed the Atlantic on the cliff-ringed shore."

WALTER DE LA MARE

" White swirled the foam, a fount,
    a blinding gleam
Of ice-cold breast, cruel eyes,
    wild mouth—and then
A still dirge echoing on from
    dream to dream."

WALTER DE LA MARE

Photo : *Frank Grattan, A.R.P.S.*

" No mystery full as Night's ; nor music
deep as the Sea's tune."

JOSEPH BRADDOCK

Photo by H. D. Keilor

LAND'S END

"On the Sea
The sunbeams tremble, and the purple light
Illumes the dark Bolerium, seat of storms."

SIR HUMPHRY DAVY

Photo : Philip Corderoy

From " CORNISH FISHER-GIRL'S SONG "

" The corn was in the shock
　And the fish were on the rock,
When the boats went out from Sennen
　　with the pilchard seine ;
　　But the morning broke so fair,
　　And not a boat was there,
And the lad I lov'd was with them and
　　he came not back again."

KATHARINE LEE JENNER

Photo : H. D. Keilo

SUNK LYONESSE

In sea-cold Lyonesse,
When the Sabbath eve shafts down
On the roofs, walls, belfries
Of the foundered town,
The Nereids pluck their lyres
Where the green translucency beats,
And with motionless eyes at gaze
Make minstrelsy in the streets.
And the ocean water stirs
In salt-worn casement and porch.
Plies the blunt-snouted fish
With fire in his skull for torch.
And the ringing wires resound ;
And the unearthly lovely weep,
In lament of the music they make
In the sullen courts of sleep :
Whose marble flowers bloome for aye :
And—tapped by the moon-guiled tide—
Mock their carver with heart of stone,
Caged in his stone-ribbed side.

WALTER DE LA MARE

Photo : *H. D. Keilor*

" Upon the cliff's warm slope
where sea-pinks grow."

MARGARET BONE

Photo : Dorien Leigh I

" A wild white welter of winnowing wings "

WALTER DE LA MARE

Photo : *Lawry Hawkey*

" In this water, clear as air,
　Lurks a lobster in its lair.
　Rock-bound weed sways out and in,
　Coral-red, and bottle-green.
　Wondrous pale anemones
　Stir like flowers in a breeze :
　Fluted scallop, whelk in shell,
　And the prowling mackerel.
　Winged with snow the sea-mews ride
　The brine-keen wind ; and far and wide
　Sounds on the hollow thunder of the tide."

WALTER DE LA MARE

" Still in chasmal beauty looms
that wild weird western shore . . ."

THOMAS HARDY